DK

The Very Hungry Caterpillar's
VERY FIRST ENCYCLOPEDIA

The Very Hungry Caterpillar's
VERY FIRST
ENCYCLOPEDIA

Contents

Our world

Body and health

Earth

Animals and nature

Penguin Random House

Editors Sally Beets, Katie Lawrence
Project Art Editor; Jacket Designer Lucy Sims
Designers Bettina Myklebust Stovne, Clare Baggaley, Hannah Moore, Sadie Thomas
US Editor Margaret Parrish
US Senior Editor Shannon Beatty
Additional Editorial Kathleen Teece

Managing Editor Jonathan Melmoth
Managing Art Editor Diane Peyton Jones
Senior Production Editor Robert Dunn
Production Controller John Casey
Picture Researcher Rituraj Singh
Publishing Coordinator Issy Walsh
Deputy Art Director Mabel Chan
Publishing Director Sarah Larter

Text Contributor Joy Evatt
Consultants John Woodward, Emily Stevenson, Yilin Wang

First American Edition, 2022
Published in the United States by DK Publishing
1450 Broadway, Suite 801, New York, New York 10018

ERIC CARLE, THE WORLD OF ERIC CARLE, THE VERY HUNGRY CATERPILLAR and certain related names and logos are registered and/or unregistered trademarks of PENGUIN RANDOM HOUSE LLC. Copyright © 2022 PENGUIN RANDOM HOUSE LLC.

History

Science, math, and technology

Space

Published in Great Britain by Dorling Kindersley Limited.

A catalog record for this book is available from the Library of Congress.
ISBN 978-0-7440-6523-7
DK books are available at special discounts when purchased in bulk for sales promotions, premiums, fund-raising, or educational use. For details, contact: DK Publishing Special Markets, 1450 Broadway, Suite 801, New York, New York 10018; SpecialSales@dk.com

Printed and bound in China

MIX
Paper | Supporting responsible forestry
FSC® C018179

This book was made with Forest Stewardship Council ™ certified paper—one small step in DK's commitment to a sustainable future.

For more information go to
www.dk.com/our-green-pledge

www.dk.com
For the curious

Our world

Where do you live?

All around the world, some people live in the **quiet countryside**, while others live in busier, **built-up places**. What kind of life do you prefer?

Life in the countryside

Not many people live in rural areas, so these places are usually quiet. There are some farms and small villages, as well as lots of open space. It can take a while to get to stores or to the hospital.

Country home

Rural houses are more spread out than city homes.

Playing outside

There are lots of open and woodland spaces to play in.

Getting around

Winding, bumpy roads can make traveling difficult.

Life in the city

Cities are places where many people live close together. There are lots of buildings, including stores, museums, schools, and hospitals.

City home
People often live in large apartment buildings.

Playing outside
There are usually playgrounds to visit.

City transportation
Trains, streetcars, buses—there are many ways to get around.

Things you do at school

School is a place where you can **learn** lots of new things. Children are taught by **teachers** in **classrooms**. It's also a place to have fun and make friends. What's your favorite thing to do at school?

Numbers
Math is all about numbers. Your teachers will help you to use math for measuring, counting, and telling time.

Learning to write
When you're ready, you'll learn to write the letters of the alphabet before spelling out words. Can you spell any words already?

Art
At school, you will try out lots of types of art. In addition to drawing and painting, you may try printmaking, jewelry-making, and creating art from paper, clay, or recycled items.

Being a good friend

At school, you will meet lots of friends. Good friends have fun playing together, are kind to each other, and help each other. Who are your best friends?

Sharing a story

Story time is special. Nonfiction books tell you amazing facts, and fiction books take you to other worlds in your imagination. Reading with a friend is a fun way to spend time together.

Playground

At school, you will have recess outside on most days. You might play games such as tag, sports such as soccer, or practice jumping rope with your friends.

11

Jobs people do

What do you want to be **when you grow up**? There are all kinds of jobs people do to find **happiness** and to earn **money**. You might want to work in a store, in a hospital, on a plane in the sky, or even at the zoo!

Teacher

When you go to school, your teacher is there to help you learn different subjects, such as math, art, science, and sports.

Doctor

Doctors help us when we are not well. They do tests to see what's wrong and give us medicine if it's needed.

Veterinarian

Vets care for and treat animals when they are sick. They might work with animals in the wild or in zoos, farm animals, or with pets.

Zookeeper

These busy workers feed, groom, and wash animals at the zoo. They make sure that the animal enclosures are neat and clean.

Sales assistant

It's the role of a sales assistant to help you find and pay for clothes, food, and other items in stores.

Pilot

Flying an airplane is a very exciting job. Pilots learn their skills using computer simulators before flying real airplanes.

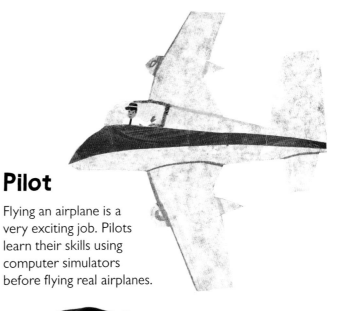

Chef

Chefs prepare food in restaurants, cafeterias, and supermarkets. What's your favorite meal?

Police officer

A police officer's job is to keep us safe and to investigate crimes.

Firefighter

Firefighters have the dangerous job of putting out fires. They also help in other tricky situations, such as car accidents or when cats get stuck up trees!

Farmer

It's the job of farmers to keep their farms running smoothly. They sell plant and animal products, such as corn and milk.

Busy at the work site

Brum-brum, chugga-chugga, beep-beep! The construction site is very **noisy**. Workers use **big machines** to lift heavy things and build new buildings.

Crane
Ropes at the end of a crane's arm lift things into the sky, such as materials to build a roof.

Dump truck
These trucks carry large amounts of material onto and off the site, such as sand and bricks.

Bulldozer
Rubble that needs to be cleared can be pushed out of the way by a bulldozer. Rubber tracks allow it to drive over bumpy ground.

Construction workers wear hard hats to protect their heads in case something falls.

14

Front-end loader

These big vehicles have a huge shovel that can be used to scoop up rocks.

Excavator

These machines dig dirt from the ground, often to make space for a foundation—the underground section of a building that makes it strong.

Backhoe loader

These tractors have a large shovel or bucket attached to the back to dig up ground, as well as one at the front.

Cement mixer

Materials can be stuck together using cement. This is made from rock and water, which are churned up in a cement mixer.

Getting around

Zoom, zoom! There are lots of different ways to travel around. Which type of **transportation** do you like the most?

Taxi

Truck

Electric car

Many modern cars now run on electricity instead of gasoline. They don't release harmful gases into the air and can power up at charging points.

Train

Trains zip through the countryside on their way from place to place. The fastest ones can go up to 190 mph (300 kph).

Space rover

Did you know there are cars on Mars? Well, sort of. Space rovers, such as *Perseverance*, rumble over the ground, taking photographs and looking for signs of life.

Bus

Bicycle

Pushing the pedals of a bike makes the wheels spin around. Don't forget to wear your helmet!

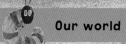

Sailing the seas

We make **boats** and **ships** so that we can **travel on water**. Here are some you might spot at sea.

Submarine

Submarines are able to hide below the surface and drop deep down to the bottom of the sea.

Container ship

These huge ships are slow but strong. They can carry lots of heavy goods at once.

Sailboat

These boats catch the wind in their sails. The harder the wind blows, the faster they move.

18

Parts of a boat

Boats have special names for their parts. The front end is called the bow and the back part is the stern. The keel is a weight under the boat that helps it stay upright. Sailboats have masts to hold up the sails.

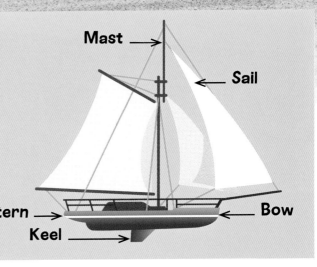

Mast

Sail

Stern

Keel

Bow

Speedboat

A speedboat has a pointed nose and a roaring engine to make it go fast. Whoosh!

Ferry

Ferries carry passengers from place to place. Some big ferries carry cars, too.

Kayak

Kayaks are small and hollow. The kayaker uses a paddle to push through the water.

Flying in the sky

Some **machines** help us **fly** up, up, and away! Have you seen any of these things in the **sky**?

Hot-air balloon

This way of flying is slow, but spectacular! The air inside is heated to make the balloon inflate and rise up into the sky.

Fighter jet

These are special planes made for armed forces. They fly very fast and are designed to fight other planes in the sky.

Helicopter

This aircraft uses its spinning blades to fly straight up and down.

How do planes fly?

When a plane moves, or thrusts forward quickly, air rushes under its wings—creating a force called lift. When this force is stronger than the force of gravity pulling it down, the plane can fly.

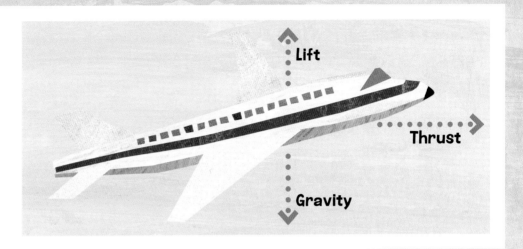

Lift

Thrust

Gravity

Parachute

Some brave people jump out of planes high in the sky. A parachute helps them float down gently and land safely on the ground.

Plane

All planes have a nose, a tail, and two wings. The pilot sits in the cockpit.

Drone

Drones are remote-controlled aircraft that don't need pilots. They can be used to take photographs, deliver packages, and more!

Hat

Pants

Socks

What we wear

What you wear each day depends on where you live and **what you are doing**. Some clothes keep you warm, while others are great for doing **activities**. What are you wearing today?

Costume

How are clothes made?

Many clothes are made by sewing pieces of fabric together. Today, this is often done by machines or by people working in factories.

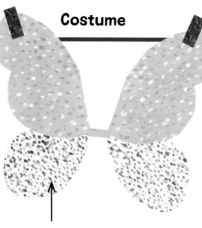

What would you pretend to be if you tried these on?

Scarf

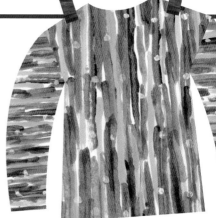

Sweater

Traditional clothes

A country's traditional clothes are called its national dress. These clothes are often worn on special occasions.

Japanese kimono

Peruvian poncho and chullo hat

Indian lehenga choli

Raincoat

Sports clothes

Shoes

What you wear on your feet depends on the weather. If it's cold, rainy, or snowy outside you might wear boots. If it's warm or dry, then sandals or sneakers are best.

Sneakers

Boots

Flip-flops

Sports clothes are made to be light and easy to move around in.

Undershirt

Skirt

Shorts

Dress

Put an undershirt on under your clothes when it's cold outside.

Samburu sashes and necklaces

Chinese hanfu

Sami gakti

23

Religion

A **set of beliefs** that a group of people share is called a religion. Religious people meet at **special buildings**, such as churches, temples, or mosques. There are many religions—let's learn about some!

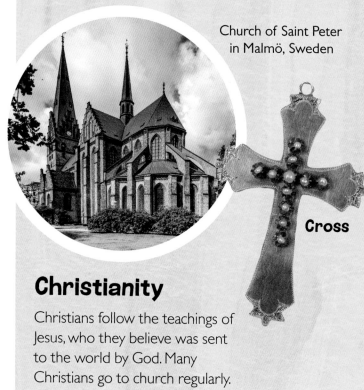

Church of Saint Peter in Malmö, Sweden

Cross

Christianity

Christians follow the teachings of Jesus, who they believe was sent to the world by God. Many Christians go to church regularly.

The Swaminarayan Mandir Hindu temple in Toronto, Canada

Judaism

Jewish people practice Judaism. They believe there is one god who made the world. The symbol of Judaism is the Star of David.

Star of David

Hinduism

People who practice Hinduism are known as Hindus. Hinduism is practiced in many places in South Asia, mostly in India.

Ganesh, a Hindu god

The Western Wall in Jerusalem, Israel

24

Wat Arun temple in Bangkok, Thailand

Buddhism

Buddhism is based on the teachings of a spiritual leader called the Buddha. The Buddha focused his teachings on ways to be happy and kind.

The Buddha

Taoism

Taoism is a way of thinking about life that began in ancient China. It teaches that balance in life is needed and this is shown in the Yin-Yang symbol.

Taiji, Yin-Yang symbol

Taoist temple, Wudang Mountains, China

Islam

People who follow Islam are known as Muslims. They believe in one god, called Allah. Every year, millions of Muslims make a special visit, or pilgrimage, to Mecca in Saudi Arabia.

Pilgrims at Mecca

Sultan Ahmed Mosque in Istanbul, Turkey

Gurdwara Bangla Sahib in New Delhi, India

Sikhism

Sikhs believe that there is one god. Sikhism is based on the teachings of 10 religious leaders called gurus. The symbol of Sikhism is the Khanda.

Khanda symbol

Let's celebrate

Lunar New Year

This 15-day festival takes place in Asian countries, such as China. There are street parades with dancers dressed up.

People celebrate for lots of different reasons—**religious festivals**, the **joy** of changing **seasons**, or to welcome a **new year**. It's time to celebrate!

Easter

Christians mark this celebration by having a special meal and going to church. People also exchange Easter eggs.

| January | February | March | April | May | June |

New Year

In many countries, people gather to celebrate the arrival of a new year at midnight on January 1. It's a time for fireworks!

Cherry Blossom Festival

This festival celebrates spring and the blossoming of cherry trees. It is celebrated in Japan.

Buddha Day

Also known as Vesak, this day celebrates the life of the Buddha.

Diwali

Diwali is the Hindu festival of lights. It is a celebration of good over evil. People light special lamps called diyas and decorate their homes with colorful patterns called rangoli.

Christmas tree

Mid-Fall Festival

This festival is celebrated in some Asian countries in the fall, when the full moon is in the sky. People make sweet-pastry moon cakes.

July	August	September	October	November	December

Eid al-Fitr

This Muslim festival marks the end of the holy month of Ramadan. People put on new clothes, pray, and exchange gifts.

New Yam Festival

Yams are eaten and people dance during this West African harvest celebration.

Christmas

During this period, Christians celebrate the birth of Jesus Christ. People give each other presents, and Christmas trees are decorated with ornaments and lights.

Halloween

This festival is celebrated in many countries across the world. People dress up in costumes, carve pumpkins, and go trick-or-treating.

Hanukkah

The Jewish people celebrate an eight-day festival called Hanukkah. They light candles each night using a special holder called a menorah to remember a great miracle.

Amazing art

Whenever you draw a picture or make a model, you are **creating art**. Artists use **different materials** to express their feelings. Here are some of the main types of art.

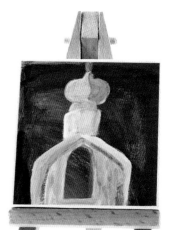

Painting

Very old cave paintings show that humans have painted since ancient times. You can paint on paper, on canvas, or even on a wall, with permission!

Drawing

It's fun to draw pictures! You can use anything that makes a mark. What are your favorite things to draw?

Sculpture

Sculptors use clay, wood, stone, metal, and other materials. Sculptures can be of familiar objects or they might be more unusual.

Collage

Collages are artworks made by sticking materials together to make a picture. Eric Carle used a paper collage technique for his illustrations!

Food around the world

Everywhere around the world, people **eat** lots of different types of food. Wherever you go, there's always **tasty** food to **try**.

Pizza

Pizza originated in Italy. Gooey cheese and fresh tomato sauce are baked on a pizza crust.

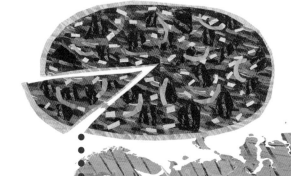

Paella

This rice-based dish comes from Spain. It's full of yummy seafood, meat, and vegetables.

Rice dishes are popular in Mali.

Tagine

This stew, often made with lamb, is from North Africa. Tagine is the name of the pot the stew is cooked in!

Kebab

Kebabs come from the Middle East. They are skewers of grilled meat and vegetables.

Cuisine

Each country, or region, has its own type of cuisine and traditional cooking methods and meals. What's your favorite type of food?

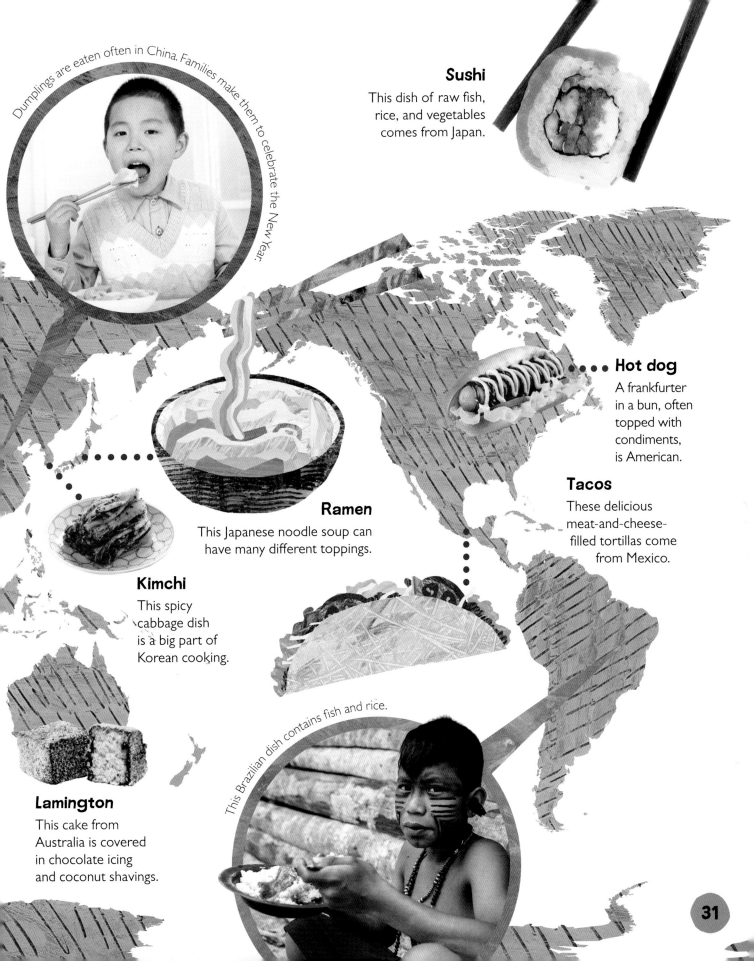

Dumplings are eaten often in China. Families make them to celebrate the New Year.

Sushi
This dish of raw fish, rice, and vegetables comes from Japan.

Hot dog
A frankfurter in a bun, often topped with condiments, is American.

Tacos
These delicious meat-and-cheese-filled tortillas come from Mexico.

Ramen
This Japanese noodle soup can have many different toppings.

Kimchi
This spicy cabbage dish is a big part of Korean cooking.

This Brazilian dish contains fish and rice.

Lamington
This cake from Australia is covered in chocolate icing and coconut shavings.

31

Marvelous music

Music can be **simple**, like clicking your fingers to a beat, or **complex**, when many musical **instruments** are played together. Do you play a musical instrument?

Brass

A musician makes sounds with a brass instrument, such as a trumpet, by using their lips. They blow into the mouthpiece to make a vibration.

Trumpet

French horn

Tuba

Woodwind

There are many types of woodwind instrument, including the recorder and saxophone. They make sound when a musician blows into the mouthpiece.

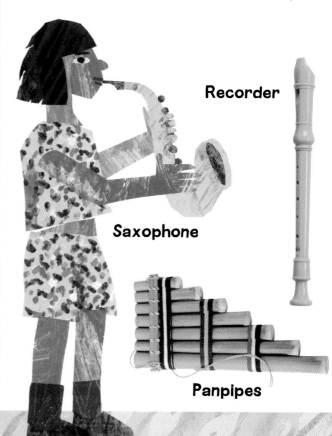

Recorder

Saxophone

Panpipes

Musical notes

Music is made up of notes. Each note is given a name, so that a tune can be written down and shared with other people to play.

C D E F G A B

Here are the notes on a piano keyboard.

String

String instruments work by making the strings vibrate, either by strumming or plucking with fingers, or by moving a bow across them.

Violin

Guitar

Pi-pa

Percussion

Percussion instruments are played by shaking and hitting them with hands or sticks. They include drums and cymbals. Some can also make tunes, such as the xylophone.

Xylophone

Tambourine

Buk drum

Sports

Sports are popular all around the world. They include team **games**, such as soccer, and **races**, such as running and cycling. A professional who plays sport is called an **athlete**.

Snowboarding

Snowboarders ride on a flat board that is attached to the rider's boots.

Swimming

Swimmers use their arms and legs to push themselves through the water.

Figure skating

Figure skaters dance on ice, balancing on sharp skates and doing jumps and spins.

Sports equipment

Equipment for sports includes special clothing, protection such as helmets, and objects such as balls and rackets.

Tennis racket and ball

Cricket ball

Boxing gloves

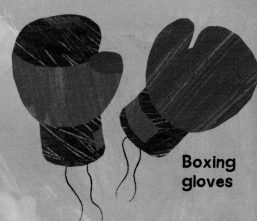

Taekwondo

In the martial art of taekwondo, people use kicks, punches, and throws.

The Olympics

The Olympic Games are the world's biggest sports competition. The very best athletes take part every four years, competing for gold, silver, and bronze medals in each event.

Soccer

Soccer players kick a ball on a grassy field. Goals are scored by kicking the ball into the other team's net.

Running

You can run on your own for exercise or against others in a race.

Basketball

In a basketball game, players try to throw the ball through a hoop at the end of the court.

Baseball glove

Referee whistle

Table tennis paddle and ball

Rugby ball

Let's talk languages

Language is how we **communicate** with each other. Imagine a world without it—you wouldn't be able to **talk** with your friends, **read** stories, or **listen** to songs. Languages are amazing!

French
Bonjour
"bon-jor"

Arabic

مرحباً
"mar-ha-ban"

Hebrew
שָׁלוֹם
"sha-lom"

Spanish
Hola
"oh-lah"

Languages

There are more than 7,000 languages across the world! Chinese is the most common one, with one billion speakers. Try saying these different greetings from around the world!

Sign language

Because deaf people can't hear sounds, they use hand signs to communicate. Letters, words, and numbers can be shown using different hand signs.

Japanese
こんにちは
"kon-nee-chee-wah"

Swedish
Hej
"hey"

Korean
안녕하세요
"ann-yeong-ha-se-yo"

Sanskrit
नमस्ते
"nah-muh-stay"

English
Hello
"hel-oh"

Chinese
你好
"nee-haow"

Braille

Braille is a way to read by moving your fingers over raised bumps. It is used by blind people all over the world.

Emojis

Emojis are little pictures that people use in messages as a quick way of expressing feelings or words. The word emoji means "picture character" in Japanese.

37

The fish is...

Little
Small
Tiny
Miniature

The whale is...

Big
Giant
Huge
Colossal

Describing words

Words that describe things are called **adjectives**.
They are really useful. Adjectives give more information
about things, such as how they look, sound, or feel.

Opposites

Opposites are things that are completely different to each other and share no similarities.

Light

Dark

Loud

Quiet

Sweet

Sour

Wonderful words

It's fun to learn new words. They give you more ways to talk about the world around you. Do you know what all of the words on this page mean?

Smooth

Strong

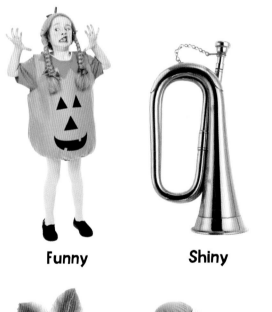

Funny

Shiny

Beautiful

Flexible

39

Body and health

Your body

Your body is amazing. It is made up of many **different parts** that help you **think, breathe, move,** and **live.**

The head

Your head is home to many of the most important parts of your body. It holds your brain, your eyes, your nose, and your mouth.

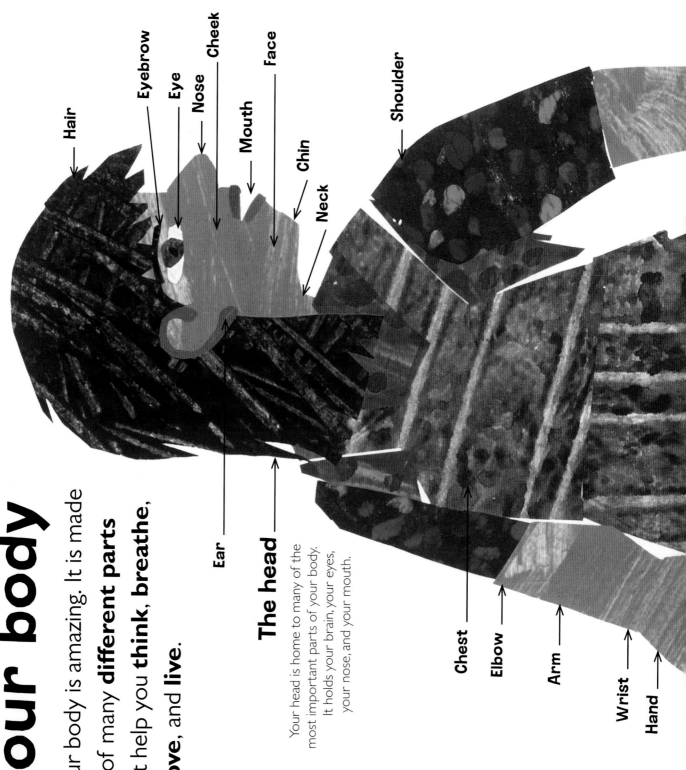

Hair

Eyebrow

Eye

Nose

Cheek

Mouth

Face

Chin

Neck

Shoulder

Ear

Chest

Elbow

Arm

Wrist

Hand

Finger

Thumb

The lower body

Joints at your hips and knees help your legs move in many different ways. That's why you can walk, run, and jump!

Ankle

Hip

Knee

Leg

Foot

Respecting others

Everyone in the world is unique. This means that no one is exactly the same. People think differently from one another, look different from each other, and act in different ways, too. It's important to respect others, even if they are different from you.

Under your skin

When you look at your **body**, you can see the **outside** of it—but there are many different things going on **inside**, too!

Believe it or not, your skin is the heaviest organ in your body!

Organs

Nose

You can spot some organs on the outside of your body, such as your eyes.

Heart

Lungs

Your kidneys help to clean your blood.

The body has many organs, all of which have different jobs to do. Your lungs help you breathe, your heart pumps blood around, and your nose allows you to smell.

Brain

The brain is a very important organ. It tells the other parts of your body what to do.

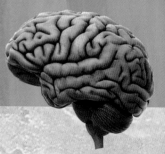

Muscles

Muscles in the face let you show different emotions.

Leg muscles help the body to run, jump, and climb.

Muscles allow you to move. The biggest muscle in the body is the gluteus maximus, which is part of the bottom!

Skeleton

The jawbone lets you open and close your mouth to eat.

Your rib cage is made of 12 pairs of bones.

The skeleton is made up of many bones, all of which are connected. Bones are strong and light. You can see bones on an X-ray image.

Special senses

Your senses help you to **explore** and **understand** the world around you. They allow you to taste, see, hear, touch, and smell.

Sight

Your eyes let you see. Light enters through the pupil—the black circle in the middle of your eye—then your brain tells you what you are seeing.

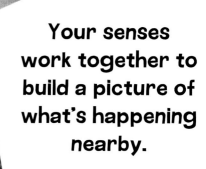

Your senses work together to build a picture of what's happening nearby.

Taste

Your tongue is covered in tiny bumps called taste buds. They tell you if food is sweet, sour, bitter, or salty.

Smell

Did you know that your nose can smell around one trillion different scents? It helps you to taste food, too.

Hearing

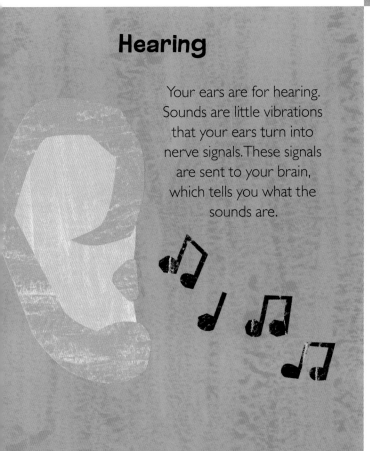

Your ears are for hearing. Sounds are little vibrations that your ears turn into nerve signals. These signals are sent to your brain, which tells you what the sounds are.

Touch

Your body uses your skin to feel things. It can tell you whether things are hot or cold, smooth or prickly, wet or dry.

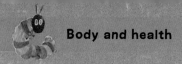

Before birth

Before babies are born, they grow inside an adult's womb for nine months. First, important organs form, such as a heart and brain. Then eyes and ears develop, and, later, nails grow on fingers and toes. All the time, the baby is getting bigger and bigger.

2 months
The size of a raspberry

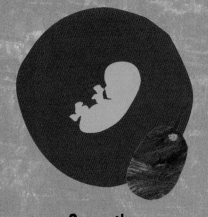

3 months
The size of a plum

How you grow

All humans are small at the start of their lives, then get bigger and **change** over time. Some adults have **children** of their own, and many go on to become grandparents. This is called the **human life cycle**.

How we age

People can look very different from each other, but all humans go through the same life stages as they get older.

2. Childhood
By this stage, a person can walk and talk. Children learn new skills at school, such as reading, writing, and playing sports.

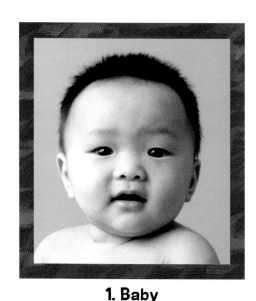

1. Baby
Babies need help from their parents to eat and stay safe. They grow quickly and soon learn to crawl and say words.

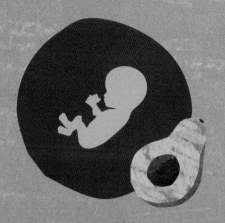

4 months
The size of an avocado

6 months
The size of a corncob

9 months
The size of
a watermelon

3. Teenager

Children become teenagers
when they are 13 years old. They
can do more things without help
from their parents, and they
start to look like adults.

4. Adulthood

Humans are fully grown
by the time they are
around 20. Adults go to
work and might now
want to have children
of their own.

5. Old age

Older people might have gray
hair or more wrinkles on their
skin. Most humans live for
more than 70 years.

A healthy plate

You need to eat a range of **different foods** to keep healthy. Some foods are good for giving you **energy**, while others help keep your body **strong**.

Orange

Lime

Kiwi

Watermelon

Carrot

Cherry

Protein

Foods that contain a lot of protein, such as meat, fish, and nuts, help your body to repair and grow.

Egg

Beans

Nuts

Meat

Fish

What's your favorite food?

Carbohydrates

Pasta, bread, rice, and potatoes are all types of carbohydrates, or carbs. They give you the energy you need to play.

Pasta

Noodles

Fruits and vegetables

Fruits and vegetables are very good for you! They keep your insides healthy. You should try to eat lots of vegetables and fruits in different colors.

Water

We need to drink lots of water to help get rid of waste and to keep our temperature normal.

Lemon

Broccoli

Pineapple

Milk

Banana

Cheese

Yogurt

Dairy

Milk, cheese, and other dairy foods can help to give you healthy bones and teeth.

Butter

Chocolate

Cake

Oil

Potatoes

Bread

Fats

Fats can give you energy. Healthy fats, such as those found in avocados and olive oil, are good for you in small amounts.

Rice

Looking after your body

From the top of your head to the tips of your toes, your **body is fantastic**. Take care of it to keep **healthy**, strong, and happy.

Brush your teeth

It's important to brush your teeth twice a day. Brush them in the front and back for two whole minutes to keep your smile sparkling and fresh.

Wash your hands

Scrub your hands with soap and water after you use the bathroom and before you eat. Make sure you wash your hands for at least 20 seconds.

Get moving!

Do you like dancing, running, cycling, or climbing? Exercising keeps your body and mind strong.

Washing

Take a shower or a bath every day to keep yourself squeaky clean.

Sleep

Your body and mind need rest to be ready for a new day. Try to sleep for at least 10 hours a night. Goodnight!

Staying safe

Safety is important because **you are important**. Let's learn about how to keep safe when you're **out and about** or at **home**.

Protect your head by wearing a helmet when you're cycling.

On the street

There is a lot to look out for when you're traveling around outside. Make sure you stay close to your grown-up, talk only to people you know, and be careful near roads.

Being safe at home

Your home should always be a safe place. But there might be some hidden dangers to be aware of, so it's a good idea to be prepared.

Electricity

We use electricity to power many things around the house. Stay away from sockets, since touching these can give you a shock.

Hot things

Watch out for anything hot, such as kettles or hot faucets. Only touch the handles of faucets or pans, so you don't burn yourself!

Hold an adult's hand and check both ways before crossing the street.

First aid

Always tell an adult if you are hurt. They might have a first-aid kit and will know how to help you.

Only cross the road where and when it is safe to do so.

Cooking

Cooking is a fun skill to learn. Make sure that you only use the oven and stovetop, electrical objects, and sharp knives with an adult's help.

Cleaning products

It's best not to touch bottles and sprays used for cleaning. They can contain chemicals that might be harmful.

Online safety

It's fun to play and learn online. But only go online with guidance from a grown-up and never talk to anyone you don't know in real life.

Emotions

You show your emotions—or feelings—through the expressions on your face. These help others know how you are. Have you ever felt the emotions these people are feeling?

Sad   **Happy**

Angry   **Scared**

Surprised   **Worried**

How do you feel?

All **feelings** are important. They begin deep inside your brain, but can affect **every part of your body**. Make sure you pay attention to how you are feeling.

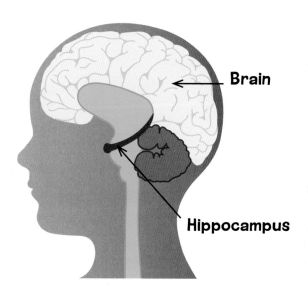

Brain

Hippocampus

Feeling afraid

When something that might be scary is going on around you, your senses send signals to a part of your brain called the hippocampus. This then sends messages to the rest of your body telling it how to react.

Friends

Pets

Sports

Reading

Painting

What makes you happy?

Music

Games

57

Feeling better

Doctors and nurses help people to stay well and to feel better when they are sick. At a **checkup**, the **doctor** will make sure that your body is healthy and growing well. Doctors often use special tools.

Stadiometer

A stadiometer has a ruler. It is used to check your height.

Doctor

Doctors work in clinics and hospitals. They treat people when they are injured or sick.

X-ray

X-ray cameras take special pictures that allow doctors to see inside the body.

58

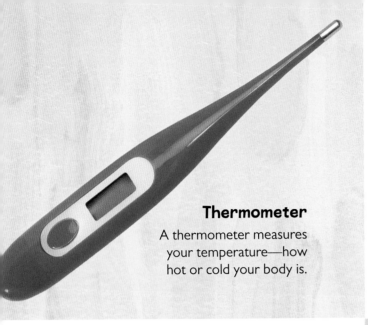

Thermometer

A thermometer measures your temperature—how hot or cold your body is.

Stethoscope

A stethoscope is a tool that lets the doctor listen to your breathing or your heartbeat.

Otoscope

Doctors use otoscopes to check inside your ears, nose, and throat.

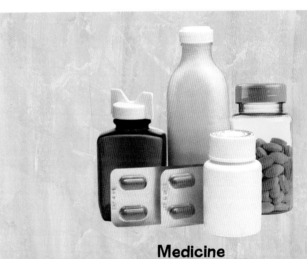

Medicine

When you get sick, a doctor might give you medicine in a tablet or liquid to help you feel better.

Bandages

If you get hurt, bandages cover the wound to keep it clean while it heals.

Ginger   Goji berries   Ginseng

Natural remedies

Some people think that certain plants make them feel better. In traditional Chinese medicine, herbs are often used to treat people.

Earth

Earth's continents

All of the land on Earth is split into seven **continents**. Each continent has a range of different landmarks, plants, animals, and peoples.

The **Golden Gate Bridge** is one of the most famous bridges in the world. It is in San Francisco, California.

North America

South America

Each continent contains many countries, except icy Antarctica.

The **Amazon Rainforest** is home to millions of species of plants and animals. Most of it is in Brazil.

62

The **Northern Lights** are beautiful green lights in the night sky. They can be seen in many northern countries.

The **Himalayas** mountain range is found in Asia. It is made up of more than 50 peaks.

Europe

Asia

Africa

Oceania

The First Australians have lived in Australia for thousands of years. There are many styles of **traditional art**, such as the one shown above.

Many tribes live in Kenya—including the **Maasai**. Each tribe has its own traditions, such as music and clothing.

Penguins

Antarctica

Asia

This is the **biggest continent**. It is home to many different **countries**, **cultures**, and **landscapes**. It is also the continent with the **most people** on it—more than half of the world's population live here.

Some important cities are marked with stars on the map. Can you spot them?

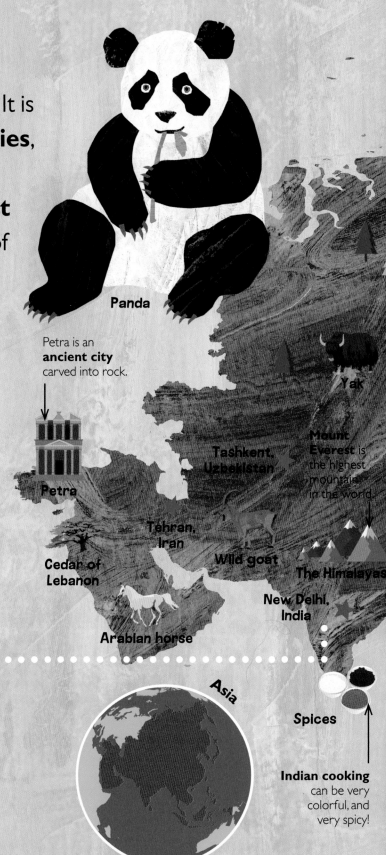

Panda

Petra is an **ancient city** carved into rock.

Petra

Yak

Tashkent, Uzbekistan

Mount Everest is the highest mountain in the world.

Tehran, Iran

Cedar of Lebanon

Wild goat

The Himalayas

New Delhi, India

Arabian horse

Asia

Spices

Indian cooking can be very colorful, and very spicy!

Taj Mahal

This beautiful domed building in India is made out of white marble. It was built in the 1600s by the emperor Shah Jahan to honor his late wife.

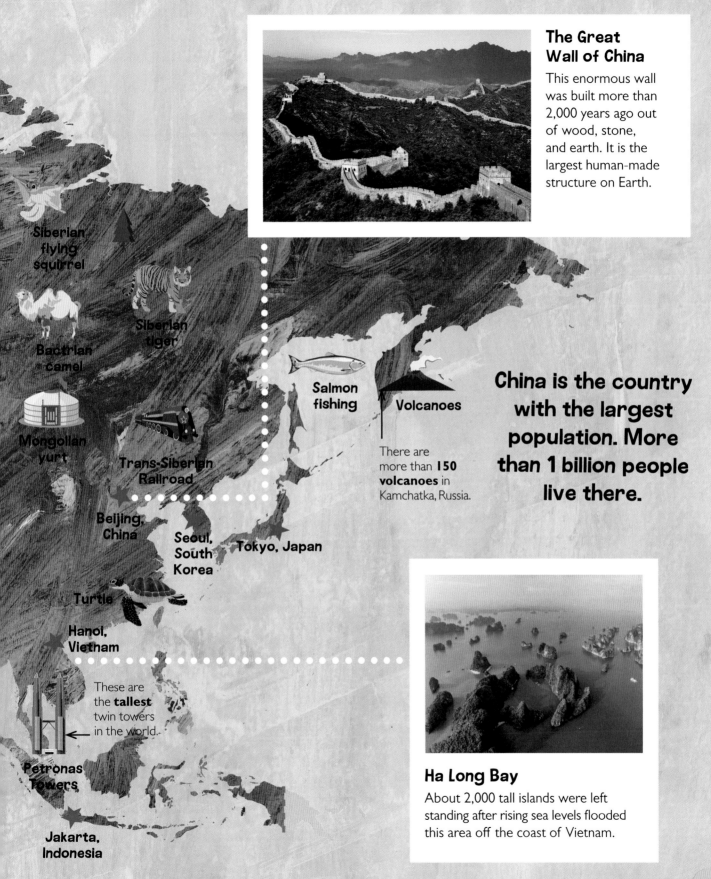

The Great Wall of China

This enormous wall was built more than 2,000 years ago out of wood, stone, and earth. It is the largest human-made structure on Earth.

Siberian flying squirrel

Bactrian camel

Siberian tiger

Mongolian yurt

Salmon fishing

Volcanoes

There are more than **150 volcanoes** in Kamchatka, Russia.

China is the country with the largest population. More than 1 billion people live there.

Trans-Siberian Railroad

Beijing, China

Seoul, South Korea

Tokyo, Japan

Turtle

Hanoi, Vietnam

These are the **tallest** twin towers in the world.

Petronas Towers

Jakarta, Indonesia

Ha Long Bay

About 2,000 tall islands were left standing after rising sea levels flooded this area off the coast of Vietnam.

North America and South America

These two continents are **linked together** by a thin strip of land. They contain tall **mountain** ranges and steamy **jungles** and are home to many amazing **animals**.

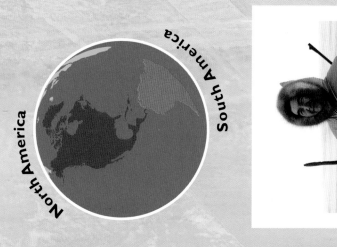

North America

South America

The Inuit

The Inuit live in the northern parts of the continent. It's very cold there, so they wear thick fur coats to stay warm.

The **Statue of Liberty** welcomes ships arriving to New York City.

Fishing boat

Moose

Ice hockey

North America

Ottawa
Canada

Washington, DC

Rocky Mountains

Rattlesnake

Sea otter

Grand Canyon

This deep valley was formed by a single river carving through rock over millions of years.

Green turtle

Mexico City, Mexico

El Castillo is a stone temple built by the Mayan people around 1,000 years ago.

The **Amazon River** holds more water than any other. It flows through the Amazon rain forest.

South America

Quito, Ecuador

On **Lake Titicaca,** local people make traditional boats out of reeds.

Toucan

The Andes

Aconcagua is the highest mountain in the Americas.

Santiago, Chile

Andean condor

Blue whale

Llama

Rio Carnival

Lasting several days, this festival in Brazil is full of dancing, parades, and music.

Machu Picchu

In the mountains of Peru sits the ancient city of Machu Picchu. It was built by the Inca people in the 1400s.

Quito, in Ecuador, is the highest capital city in the world.

Patagonia

At the southern tip of South America is a wild region called Patagonia. Icy glaciers (huge rivers of ice) slide down mountains, and freezing winds blow over from nearby Antarctica.

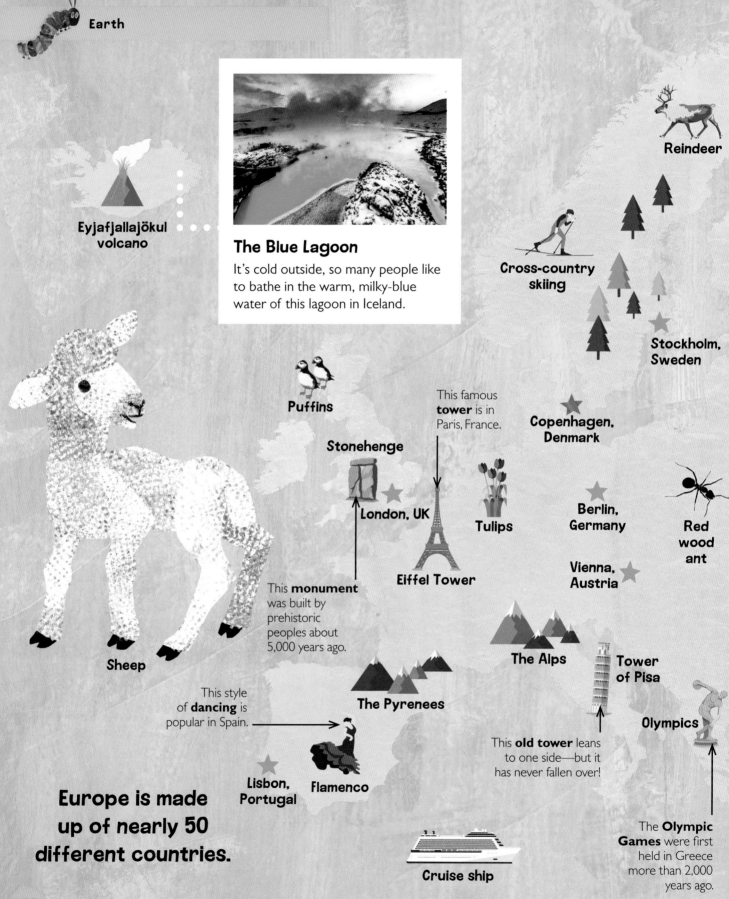

The Blue Lagoon
It's cold outside, so many people like to bathe in the warm, milky-blue water of this lagoon in Iceland.

Eyjafjallajökul volcano

Reindeer

Cross-country skiing

Stockholm, Sweden

Puffins

This famous **tower** is in Paris, France.

Stonehenge

Copenhagen, Denmark

London, UK

Tulips

Berlin, Germany

Red wood ant

Eiffel Tower

Vienna, Austria

This **monument** was built by prehistoric peoples about 5,000 years ago.

Sheep

The Alps

Tower of Pisa

This style of **dancing** is popular in Spain.

The Pyrenees

Olympics

Lisbon, Portugal

Flamenco

This **old tower** leans to one side—but it has never fallen over!

Europe is made up of nearly 50 different countries.

Cruise ship

The **Olympic Games** were first held in Greece more than 2,000 years ago.

Mountain hare

These **jeweled eggs** were made for the Russian rulers.

Fabergé egg

European bison

This is often used as a **Christmas tree** in Europe.

Norway spruce

Wolverine

Brown bear

Golden eagle

The Ural Mountains

This mountain range in Russia is part of the border between Europe and Asia.

Moscow, Russia

Wild boar

Kiev, Ukraine

Beach resorts

Balalaika

St. Basil's Cathedral

This famous building in Moscow, Russia, is more than 450 years old. Its onion-shaped domes are painted in bright colors.

Mount Elbrus

Monk seal

Europe

Europe

This continent has many **countries** and **languages**. In the cold north there are forests and icy lakes, while in the south it is warm and sunny.

Africa

This enormous continent is the **second largest** in the world. In Africa, you can find **rain forests**, **deserts**, **lakes**, and **grasslands**. It also has the world's largest desert, the Sahara.

Marrakech

This city in Morocco is famous for its bustling markets, which sell spices, jewelry, and leather.

The buildings in this fort are made of **red mud-bricks**. →

Ait Benhaddou

Sahara Desert

Bananas

← Fruit grows well in the **hot jungles** of West Africa.

Accra, Ghana

Africa

Victoria Falls

This huge waterfall lies on the border between Zambia and Zimbabwe. It is one of the largest waterfalls in the world.

Giraffe

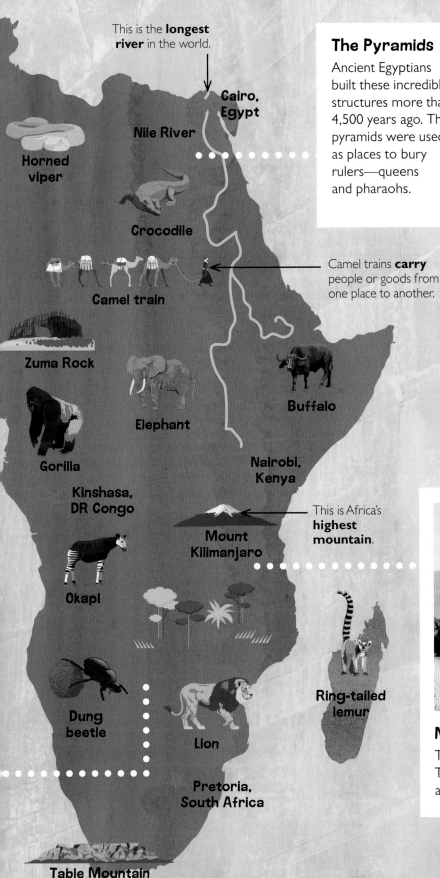

This is the **longest river** in the world.

Horned viper

Cairo, Egypt

Nile River

Crocodile

Camel train

Camel trains **carry** people or goods from one place to another.

Zuma Rock

Elephant

Buffalo

Gorilla

Nairobi, Kenya

Kinshasa, DR Congo

Okapi

Mount Kilimanjaro

This is Africa's **highest mountain**.

Dung beetle

Lion

Ring-tailed lemur

Pretoria, South Africa

Table Mountain

The Pyramids

Ancient Egyptians built these incredible structures more than 4,500 years ago. The pyramids were used as places to bury rulers—queens and pharaohs.

The first humans lived in southern Africa millions of years ago.

National parks

There are many national parks in Africa. They are home to hundreds of different animals—can you spot some on the map?

Oceania

Far away from the other continents, Oceania is home to many **unique animals**. In the **warm waters** surrounding the many islands of the region are beautiful, colorful **coral reefs**.

This island is split between two continents. The eastern part is in **Oceania**, and the western part is in Asia.

Kangaroo

Bearded dragon

Crocodile

Australia is the **largest country** in Oceania.

Uluru

Dingo

A colorful **gemstone** found in some rocks

Opal

Quokkas

These adorable animals are found in western Australia. Mother quokkas keep new babies inside a special belly pouch, like kangaroos.

Indian Pacific Railway

This **railroad** runs all the way across Australia.

Oceania

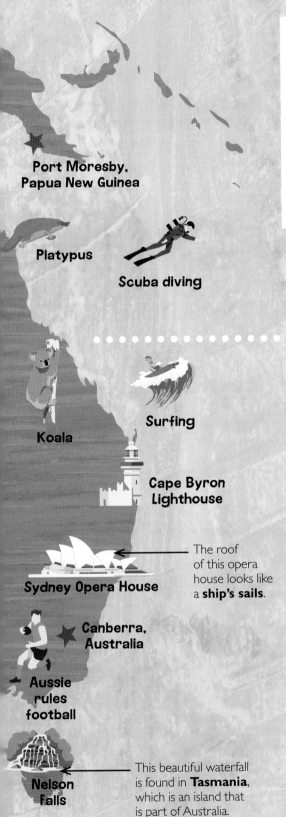

Port Moresby,
Papua New Guinea

Platypus

Scuba diving

Koala

Surfing

Sharks

Cape Byron
Lighthouse

The roof
of this opera
house looks like
a **ship's sails**.

Sydney Opera House

Canberra,
Australia

Aussie
rules
football

This beautiful waterfall
is found in **Tasmania**,
which is an island that
is part of Australia.

Nelson
Falls

The Great Barrier Reef

Stacks of animals called corals make up reefs, and bright fish swim among them. The Great Barrier Reef is the biggest coral reef on Earth.

The All Blacks

New Zealand's rugby team is the All Blacks—one of the best rugby teams in the world. Their uniform is black and players perform the haka, the traditional Maori war dance, before every match.

The **Maori people** have lived in Aotearoa (now known as New Zealand) for around 700 years.

Maori
meeting
house

Kiwi

Wellington,
New Zealand

There are more than 10,000 islands in Oceania.

Yellow-eyed
penguin

Earth's structure

Our amazing planet is a huge sphere made up of five main **layers**. We live on top of the thin outer layer. Deep inside the Earth is **liquid rock**.

You would have to dig down 4,000 miles (6,400 km) to reach the center of the Earth.

Crust →
The crust is Earth's top layer and its outer shell. It is mostly made of solid rock.

Upper mantle —
The upper mantle is attached to the crust. It contains solid and liquid, or molten, hot rock.

Lower mantle
This layer is made of hot solid rock. It is thicker than the upper mantle.

Outer core
The outer core is made of moving and flowing hot liquid metal.

Inner core
The very center of our planet is made of hot solid metal.

Types of crust

The crust is the surface of planet Earth. There are two different types of crust because it makes up the Earth's land and also covers the ocean floor.

Oceanic crust

The oceanic crust is a thin part of the Earth's crust under the ocean.

Continental crust

The continental crust makes up the dry land where we live.

Earth has many layers, like an onion.

The inner core is as hot as the surface of the sun.

Inside a volcano

Burning hot-molten rock collects inside a volcano in an area called a magma chamber. The magma either cools and becomes rock or erupts to become lava.

Magma chamber

Eruption

When a volcano erupts, hot magma rises up and bursts through an opening in the top of the volcano.

Volcanoes

Volcanoes are incredible, but dangerous. They are huge **mountains** filled with scorching molten rock called **magma**. When a volcano erupts, fiery magma spurts into the air.

Ash cloud

Little pieces of rock and magma burst out of volcanoes in huge smoky clouds during an eruption. The ash can travel so far that it can affect the weather all around the world.

Lava

When hot magma erupts from a volcano, it is called lava. It can shoot high into the air like a fountain, then flow down the volcano in rivers. When it cools, it becomes rock.

Types of volcano

Active volcano

If a volcano has erupted within the last 10,000 years, it's called "active." It might erupt at any time.

Dormant volcano

A dormant volcano might erupt again one day.

Extinct volcano

An extinct volcano is one that has not erupted in a very long time and scientists believe won't erupt again.

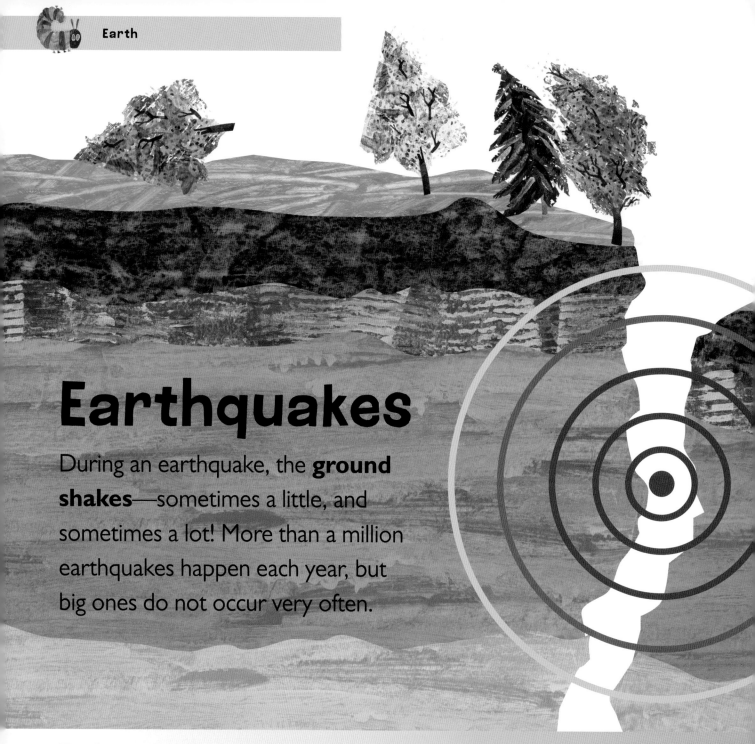

Earthquakes

During an earthquake, the **ground shakes**—sometimes a little, and sometimes a lot! More than a million earthquakes happen each year, but big ones do not occur very often.

Richter scale

1　　　**2**　　　**3**

The strength of an earthquake is measured using the Richter scale, invented by an American scientist in 1934. The higher the number, the stronger the earthquake.

Low

People usually cannot feel very small earthquakes, which are less than 3 on the scale.

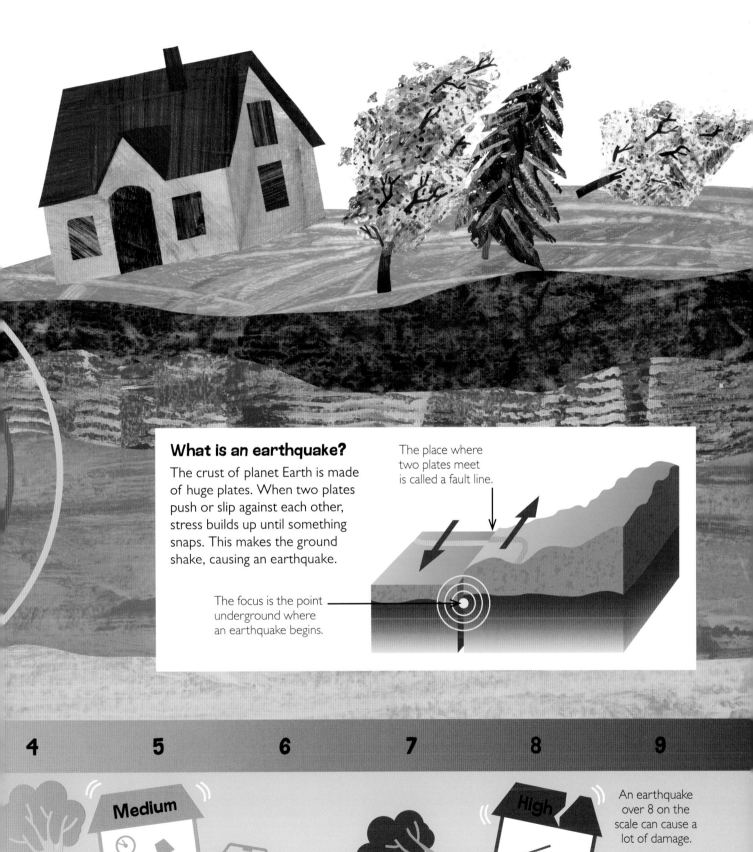

What is an earthquake?

The crust of planet Earth is made of huge plates. When two plates push or slip against each other, stress builds up until something snaps. This makes the ground shake, causing an earthquake.

The place where two plates meet is called a fault line.

The focus is the point underground where an earthquake begins.

4   5   6   7   8   9

Medium

High

An earthquake over 8 on the scale can cause a lot of damage.

Top of the world

Mountains are found all around the world. These **tall peaks** are often covered in **snow** at the top, even in the summer. They usually have very steep sides and tower over the surrounding landscape.

Mount Kilimanjaro

Africa's highest mountain is Mount Kilimanjaro. It is actually a volcano, although it hasn't erupted in a very long time.

Mount Elbrus

This mountain is the tallest peak in Russia and Europe. The top of it is permanently covered in snow.

Mount Kilimanjaro, Tanzania
19,340 ft (5,895 m)

Mount Elbrus, Russia
18,510 ft (5,642 m)

Vinson Massif, Antarctica
16,023 ft (4,897 m)

How are mountains made?

Mountains are made when parts of the Earth's crust, called plates, bump into each other.

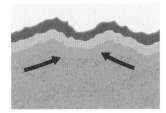

Fold mountain

Most mountains are fold mountains. They are made when plates slowly push together, making folds.

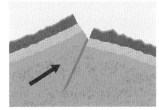

Block mountain

Block mountains are formed along a crack in Earth's crust when some rock is pushed up and some is pushed down.

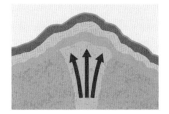

Dome mountain

When hot liquid rock inside Earth pushes the ground upward, it forms a dome mountain.

Tallest mountain

The world's highest mountain is Mount Everest, on the China-Nepal border. More than 4,000 brave climbers have reached the top of Everest.

Mount Everest, China-Nepal border
29,029 ft (8,848 m)

Aconcagua, Argentina
22,834 ft (6,960 m)

Denali, USA
22,310 ft (6,190 m)

81

Under the sea

The oceans are much **bigger than they look** because the water is so deep. Shallow parts are warm and filled with light; farther down, it's dark and cold. You'll find different **living things** at each level.

Sunlit zone

The top ocean layer contains the majority of plants and animals. It receives the most sunlight, so is the warmest.

Twilight zone

Not much sunlight reaches this deep, so plants don't grow here. There are still fish and animals, but many of them swim up to the sunlit zone to find food.

Midnight zone

Creatures such as starfish stick to the seabed. →

No light reaches the deepest parts of the ocean. Weird and wonderful creatures lurk here. The water is dark, except for some animals that glow.

29 percent land

71 percent water

Watery world

Our world is known as the "blue planet." This is because it's covered in so much water.

It's easy to see how the swordfish got its name. It has a long, sharp nose, which it uses to attack other fish.

Sea or ocean?

Earth has five main oceans and many smaller seas. Seas are smaller than oceans and are usually close to land. You can't drink any of the water contained in oceans and seas—it's too salty!

At the very bottom of the ocean you find the hadal zone. Very few creatures live here in the total darkness.

In the desert

Most people think of deserts as vast areas of scorching heat and sand, but deserts are really just places where it **hardly ever rains**. They can be hot or cold, inland or by the sea.

Sahara Desert

Hot deserts

With cloudless skies above, desert days can be very hot, but at night they become cold. The Sahara in Africa is the hottest desert in the world.

Cheetah

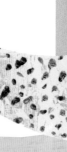

Palm tree

In the desert

Over thousands of years, different features can be formed in deserts. Strong winds, heat, and water will all carve and shape the land.

Oasis

An oasis is a place in the desert that has water, trees, and plants.

84

Gobi Desert

Atacama Desert

Cold deserts

Cold deserts change temperature with the seasons. The Gobi Desert in Asia reaches -40°F (-40°C) in winter, which is about twice as cold as a freezer!

Coastal deserts

Found where the ocean meets land, coastal deserts can go years without rain. However, the cold air from the ocean often creates thick fog.

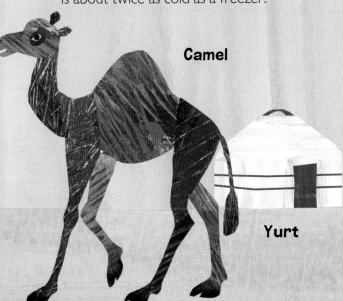

Camel

Yurt

Flamingo

Cactus

Sand-storm

A sandstorm blows huge clouds of debris around the desert.

Buttes

Flat-topped hills with steep sides are known as buttes.

Rocks and minerals

Rocks are formed from tiny grains of **minerals** (natural nonliving substances). There are many types of rock—some are **hard**, while some are **soft** and crumbly.

The igneous rock obsidian is known as "nature's glass."

Igneous rocks

These rocks are made when magma (hot molten rock) cools down. They form underground, or after a volcano erupts.

Granite bridge

Fossils are mostly found in sedimentary rocks.

Sedimentary rocks

Sedimentary rocks are made when wind or rain breaks rocks into tiny pieces and these pieces are packed together. This type of rock includes limestone and sandstone.

Limestone cliffs

Diggers help us find rocks and minerals in the ground.

Marble is made from limestone and minerals.

Metamorphic rocks

These types of rock are formed when sedimentary or igneous rocks are heated up and squeezed, causing them to change into metamorphic rocks.

Marble statue

Gemstones

Gemstones are hard, colorful crystals formed from minerals. They are found by digging into the ground. They can be cut, polished, and used for jewelry.

Red mineral
Garnet

Yellow mineral
Pyrite

White mineral
Moonstone

Green mineral
Jade

Blue/green mineral
Turquoise

Purple mineral
Amethyst

87

Wonderful water

Have you ever wondered where rain comes from? **Water is constantly moving**. It flows to the sea, rises in the air, then falls as rain. This is called the water cycle.

2. Making clouds

As the water vapor rises, it starts to cool again and turns into tiny water droplets. These collect together to make clouds.

1. Water vapor

The sun heats the surface of the sea. This causes the water to change from a liquid to a gas, called water vapor, which rises from the sea.

3. Falling rain

When the clouds get heavier than the air around them, the water falls as rain, snow, or hail.

Types of water

Saltwater

Saltwater is found in oceans and seas. It's too salty to drink, but is easier to float in than fresh water.

Fresh water

You find fresh water in rivers, lakes, and streams. Most fresh water, however, is actually frozen as ice.

4. Back to the sea

Rainwater trickles into streams and flows in rivers before returning to the sea, where the cycle begins again.

What is weather?

Rainy or windy, hot or cold, snowy or sunny—weather is the name for what is **happening in the air** around us. What's your favorite type of weather?

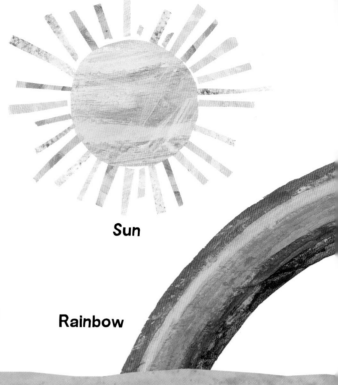

Sun

Rainbow

How weather happens

Weather occurs when air gets warmer or cooler. It then moves around Earth's atmosphere, making wind and rain.

Getting dressed

Which of these items would you wear in wet, cold weather? How about if it were hot and sunny?

Rain

Snow

Wind

Wild weather

Extreme weather events, such as big storms, can cause floods, fires, and a lot of damage.

Thunderstorms

These noisy storms can be quite spectacular. Thunder and lightning happen when electricity shoots down from a cloud, making the air heat up and creating a rumbling sound.

Tornadoes

Twisting tornadoes are superfast winds that spin in a circle. They can flip over cars and tear up trees.

Winter

Brr, it's cold in this season!
Snow might fall, and
slippery ice can cover
puddles and ponds. Many
trees lose their leaves.

Seasons

The **weather** changes
throughout the year—and you
can spot **nature changing**
with it! In many parts of the
world, there are four seasons.

Spring

The weather gets
a little warmer in
spring. Leaves and
colorful blossoms
sprout from some
trees, and lots of
animals are born.

Summer

The sun shines the most in summer. Many flowers bloom to soak up its light, and fruit ripens on certain trees.

Fall

In this season, the leaves of many trees turn golden and drop off. It gets colder, and some animals go into sleeplike hibernation.

Two seasons

Tropical countries are near the equator, which is an invisible band that goes around the middle of the Earth. In these places, the temperature stays warm all year. There are just two seasons—a dry season and a very rainy season, sometimes called a monsoon.

Tropical rain

Protecting the planet

Our world provides us with all we need to survive, but these resources are not endless. **Small changes** can help us to look after our world.

Reuse and recycle

When we throw stuff away, it doesn't just disappear. Much of it is burned or dumped, but some can be recycled. Recycling means turning waste into something new!

Avoid plastics

Plastic is a big problem. It's very difficult to get rid of and is harmful to animals. Talk to your parents about swapping plastic bags for reusable ones and ask for wooden or recycled toys for your birthday.

The world is getting hotter

Technology, factories, and transportation need lots of energy to run. Creating this energy releases gases into the air that are making the planet hotter. This is having a dangerous effect on animals and nature—including causing ice to melt in the polar regions.

Walk and cycle more

Using vehicles releases harmful gases. It's great to get into the habit of getting out and about without using a car. Whether you and your family walk, cycle, scoot, or roller blade, you can have fun getting around at the same time as taking care of our planet.

Spread the word!

Tell others about the importance of keeping our world healthy! Make a poster to put in your window, start a gardening club, or organize a litter-pickup with your family.

Garden

Growing plants at home or school helps to keep the air healthy. This is because plants produce the gas oxygen, which we use to breathe.

Animals
and nature

What is alive?

All around us there are living things, from the **birds** and **trees** in the woods to the **flowers** and tiny **insects** in our gardens. But what does it mean to be alive?

Living things

Living things breathe, grow, eat, move, and make new life. Animals have babies and plants make seeds.

Animals

An animal is a living creature, such as a fish, cat, or gorilla.

Living things

Breathe

Grow and die

Need food

Need water

Plants

Plants are living things, such as grass, flowers, and trees, that cover the land.

How are plants and animals different?

Animals can do things that plants cannot. They move around and they are aware of the world around them. Animals also need to eat plants and other animals to stay alive.

If you find a mushroom in the wild, just look and don't touch. It could be poisonous.

Fungi

Mushrooms and molds are types of fungi. Fungi feed on living or dead plants and animals.

Nonliving things

Our planet is full of nonliving things that help plants and animals survive. Some are natural and some are human-made.

Water

From the smallest ants to the largest elephants, all life needs water to survive.

Light

Light is important for all living things. Plants use the sun to create food.

Human-made things

Many objects that fill our world, such as this plastic shovel, are made by humans.

Soil

Plants need soil to live. They grow roots in soil to help them stand up and to soak up water and food.

Minerals

Minerals are substances found in rocks and soil. Plants use some minerals as food to grow.

Flower

Plants and trees

Every day, we see plants growing in our **gardens**, **parks**, and pots inside our **homes**. Plants give us fruits, vegetables, medicines, and materials for clothes.

Leaves

Stem

Roots

Flowers

Flowers are the colorful parts of plants. You will often see bees buzzing around them.

Ferns

Instead of seeds, green and leafy ferns have spores under their leaves that look like little dots.

Conifers

Trees that make woody cones are called conifers.

Plants

Plants come in all colors, shapes, and sizes. They provide homes and food for living things.

Moss

Moss looks like a soft, green rug growing on trees, rocks, and on the ground.

Flowering trees

Flowering trees bloom in the springtime. They create beautiful bursts of color, called blossom, in streets and gardens.

Evergreen

Trees that stay green all year round are called evergreen trees.

Deciduous

In the fall, the leaves of deciduous trees turn orange, red, or brown and fall to the ground.

Apple tree

Trees

Trees are very tall plants. They have leaves, branches, and thick stems called trunks. Trees can live for thousands of years.

Fruit trees

Many trees grow fruit that we can eat, such as apples, pears, oranges, and plums.

101

How do plants grow?

A plant starts its life as a tiny **seed**. Plants need **food** to grow, just like us. They create their food using the sun up above and the soggy soil down below. Their **roots** dig deep into the ground to suck up water.

How do seeds spread?

Seeds are little packages that contain everything a plant needs to grow. Some seeds are very light and shaped to float easily. They can spread to new locations in the wind. Others are carried by insects and animals.

3. Shoot grows

A young plant, or seedling, sprouts out of the ground. The short shoot straightens up toward the sunlight.

2. Breaking open

The plant's first root begins to grow down into the soil. The root's tiny hairs help it to take in water.

1. Seed

When a single seed begins to grow, it is called germination. The seed soaks up water and, as it gets bigger, its coat splits.

5. Fully grown

The plant is fully grown. Some plants live for a few months and others for hundreds of years.

4. Leaves sprout

The plant's leaves turn to face the sun. Some plants also grow flowers or fruit.

Seeds will start to grow into plants when they have enough water and sunlight.

Plants produce the gas oxygen, which animals (like us!) use to breathe.

Plants take in carbon dioxide gas from the air.

Photosynthesis

Plants make their own food through a process called photosynthesis. Their leaves get energy from the sunlight and use it to turn water and a gas called carbon dioxide into sugars.

Plants take in water from the soil.

All about animals

From big blue whales to little ladybugs, our world is full of fascinating animals. They all have special **features** that help them to **survive** where they live. There are many animal types that are often split into **six main groups**.

Reptiles

Covered in tough, scaly skin, reptiles include snakes, crocodiles, and lizards. Most reptiles lay eggs.

Chameleons can change the color of their skin. This can help them to blend in with their leafy surroundings.

Frogs launch themselves into the air using their strong back legs.

Invertebrates

These animals don't have backbones. They include insects, jellyfish, and worms. Octopuses are also invertebrates!

Spiders have eight spindly legs. They make silk and use it to weave webs.

Amphibians

Newts, frogs, and toads are all amphibians. They are cold-blooded and can live both in water and on land.

How do birds fly?

Most birds are natural-born fliers. They flap their wings to thrust forward using their strong chest muscles. Birds also have air inside their bones. This makes them light enough to fly.

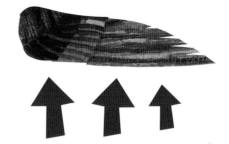

When a bird flies, something called air pressure is created below its wings. This pushes the bird up.

Mammals

Did you know that we humans are mammals? All mammals have hair or fur. Newborns feed on their mother's milk.

Tropical birds are colorful and often very noisy.

Tigers are big, strong cats. Each tiger's fur has its own unique stripe pattern.

Birds

Some birds can fly, some can talk, but they all have feathers and beaks. You find them all over the world.

Fish

Many of these watery creatures are covered in scales, which protect them. Fish breathe underwater by using their gills.

Fish have flapping fins and smooth shapes to help them glide through the water. Many live on coral reefs.

Animals at home

Some animals are wild, but other, tamer creatures make perfect **pets**. A dog, a cat, a fish, a hamster—if you could have any pet, what would it be?

Fish

Make sure you have a nice big tank for fish, so they have lots of space to swim around.

Goldfish are the most popular pet fish.

Rabbits

Rabbits get lonely, so it's best to keep them in pairs. Some pet rabbits live inside, others in a hutch outdoors.

Tortoise

If you want a pet tortoise, think carefully, as some types can grow to be huge and live for more than 50 years!

Caring for your pet

Pets are lots of fun, but they need to be cared for. Every pet needs somewhere safe and clean to live, fresh food and water, space to play, and lots of love—just like you!

Water

Bed

Somewhere to exercise

Hamster

Food

Humans first kept cats as pets around 12,000 years ago!

Dog

These playful animals are very popular pets. They need to be fed and walked regularly.

Cat

Cats are creatures of comfort. Most cats love being stroked and will purr when relaxed.

On the farm

Farms are **busy** places. Farmers get up **early** to feed the animals, lay out hay, and plow the fields. It's **hard work**!

Tractor

Horse

On many farms, horses help out by carrying farmers on their backs or pulling heavy loads.

Hay

Pig

Oink, oink! Pigs love to roll around in the mud. It keeps them cool and protects them from the sun.

108

Barn

Crops

Many farms grow crops such as wheat, corn, and rice in large fields. Rice is grown in hot countries in water-covered areas called paddy fields.

Sheep

What noise do sheep make? Their thick coats are sheared off to make woolen clothes for us to wear.

Cow

Moo! Cows produce milk, which can then be made into cheese.

Chicken

Chickens lay about one egg a day. They sit on their eggs to keep them safe and warm.

Wetland wildlife

Bogs, marshes, and swamps are places where the ground is **soaked in water**. These fascinating areas are home to many animals that live in water, such as **fish**, **birds**, **frogs**, and **reptiles**.

Bogland

The ground here is very soft and spongy because it is made of dead and dying plants soaked in rainwater.

Shallow-water wetland

These wetlands are like shallow ponds with pretty floating plants, such as water lilies. The water comes from rain or small streams.

Frogs lay their eggs in water.

Hippos stay cool by relaxing in water.

The Pantanal

One of the largest wetlands is the Pantanal, which crosses three countries in South America. Many exotic animals live there, such as jaguars, anteaters, and giant otters.

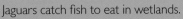
Jaguars catch fish to eat in wetlands.

Marshland

Marshes have shallow pools of water that are full of small plants, such as reeds, grasses, and herbs. These areas can be found near seas, lakes, or rivers.

Grass snakes hide in tall grasses looking for animals to hunt.

Swampland

Swamps have deep water. They are covered in trees and plants, making them a popular place for animals to nest.

Alligators hunt for food in water.

What is a forest?

A forest is an area of land with many trees. There are different types of forest all around the world, and they are full of plants and animals.

Coniferous forest

In cooler parts of the world, trees in coniferous forests have needlelike leaves that stay green all year round.

Conifer tree needles can be soft or spiked.

Found in the forest

Walking through a forest is a magical experience. Look up at the trees and down by your feet to explore the many different **plants** and **animals** around you.

Fox

Fungi

Badger

112

Deciduous forest

In the spring, the deciduous forest comes alive with colorful flowers, insects, and birds. In the fall, the trees lose their leaves.

Leaves come in many shapes and colors.

Woodpecker

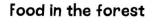

Bear

Food in the forest

Animals can find lots to eat on the forest floor and in trees and bushes. There are often plenty of tasty berries and nuts!

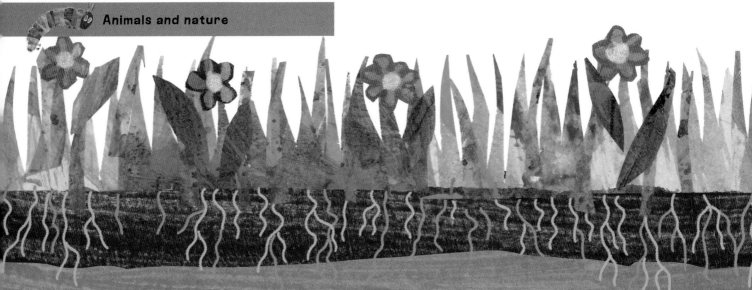

Under the ground

So much goes on beneath the **soil**. Plants grow **roots**, small animals **burrow**, and millions of creepy-crawlies search around **looking for meals**.

Worm
These wriggly wonders have long, soft bodies and no legs.

Millipede
Millipedes have many legs that create a wave motion when they walk. They bulldoze their way through the ground, using their legs to push them forward.

Slug
Slugs like to lurk in damp places, which is why you often see them after it rains. They leave a sticky, slimy trail behind them.

Putting down roots
Plants grow roots to secure them in the ground and to draw up water for food. The roots spread out below them in a tangled web.

Marvelous minis

Creepy-crawlies make up the biggest group of animals on Earth. Most of them are very little and like the cool, dark, and damp conditions under the ground.

Mole

These brilliant burrowers spend most of their time digging a maze of tunnels, looking for creepy-crawlies to munch on.

Ants

Amazing ants work together in huge groups to carry food through hidden underground tunnels.

Beetle

Beetles are the most common type of bug. Hard outer wings protect the wings they use to fly.

Creatures on the coast

Wherever you are in the world, take a walk along the **beach** and you'll find many different **seabirds** and other interesting animals.

Seagull

Beaches

Many animals like to use the sand, rocks, and plants at the beach for their nests. These include seagulls, seals, and sea turtles.

Sea

Sand

Pelican

Seal

What are tides?

The water level at the coast goes up and down. This is called the tide. At low tide, the beach is dry. At high tide, the beach is underwater.

High tide

Low tide

Sea turtles bury their eggs in deep holes on sandy beaches.

Sea turtle

Crab

Rock pools

Rock pools at the beach can give us a wonderful view into the world of sea creatures and plants. These pools are left behind when the tide goes out.

Seaweed   **Fish**   **Starfish**   **Anemone**

School of fish

Sometimes fish and other sea creatures swim together in beautiful sweeping shapes. We call these schools.

Sea creatures

There is a colorful, vibrant world **under the sea**. It is home to many animal types. Some are big, some are small, some are spiny, and others are scaly!

Shark

With sharp teeth and powerful tails, sharks are the best hunters in the ocean. The biggest shark is 60 ft (18 m) long, the length of two buses!

Seahorse

Tiny, spiny seahorses are fish that swim upright in shallow waters. The males carry their babies in pouches on their fronts.

The bottom of the sea is called the seafloor or the seabed.

Dolphin

Lively dolphins leap and play in the ocean. They live in groups called pods and talk to their friends in whistles and clicks.

Manatee

Sometimes called sea cows, manatees are large plant-eating animals. These peaceful creatures relax in shallow waters.

Jellyfish

Jellyfish are soft sea creatures that float and drift with ocean currents. They have long, stinging tentacles.

Coral reef

A colorful wonderland, a coral reef is built by living animals called corals. These catch tiny floating creatures for food with their tentacles. But the warm, shallow waters of the reef also provide a home for many other animals.

Starfish

Covered in suckers, these star-shaped sea creatures eat smaller animals, such as snails, clams, and oysters.

Mountain life

It's cold, windy, and there isn't much **food**
to eat or **air** to breathe in the mountains.
These amazing animals manage to
survive in the **harsh conditions**.

Red panda

Red pandas look like
a mix between a
bear and a panda,
but they are actually
related to raccoons.

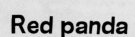

Llama

Light-footed llamas
are experts at
climbing up steep
mountain paths.

Mountain goat

Mountain goats are covered in
thick fur to keep them warm.
Their padded hooves help them
to leap across mountain rocks.

120

Andean condor

Found in the Andes Mountains of South America, this creature is the largest bird in the world.

Keeping warm

Japanese macaques, also called snow monkeys, take dips in hot springs to stay warm. They also cuddle together for warmth, just like humans.

Snow leopard

This big cat has wide, spongy paws for gripping onto the ice. It's difficult to spot snow leopards because they blend into the snowy slopes.

Yak

Yaks are horned animals from the cow family. They have a hairy, two-layered coat. The outer layer is waterproof, and the inner layer keeps them nice and warm.

Desert animals

Life can be **tough** for animals that live in deserts. It can get very **hot** and there is **little water**. Desert-dwelling creatures have special ways of staying cool, finding water, and surviving.

Camel

Camels have fat stored in their humps. This allows them to go days without food or water.

Jerboa

Jerboas stay cool by making small burrows in the desert.

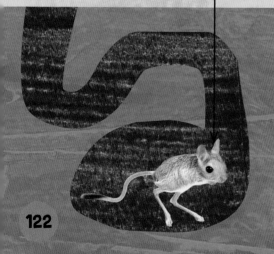

Staying alive

Desert animals have special features that help them to stay alive. Some features keep them cool, while others are for protection or attack.

Fennec fox

The fluffy fennec fox has huge ears. These let heat escape from its body and help keep it cool.

Eagle

With their powerful claws and flying skills, eagles are expert hunters.

Gazelle

The speedy gazelle can go months without drinking water. It gets water from plants instead.

Lizard

You find all sorts of lizards in the desert. The sand is scorching, but lizards move quickly so their feet don't burn.

Viper

Look out! Vipers wind their way through the sand. Their coloring helps them to blend in and surprise animals when they attack!

Thorny devil

Ouch! This is a prickly animal! The thorny devil has sharp spines, which makes it hard for other animals to catch and eat it.

Scorpion

If a scorpion lifts up its tail, watch out—it's ready to attack! It has a deadly stinger at the tip.

123

Polar animals

The **North** and **South poles** are found on opposite sides of the world. The **polar** regions are incredibly **cold**, but they're still home to some hardy animals.

Arctic hare

Quick runners, these bouncy animals have big feet that help them to reach speeds of up to 40 mph (65 kph)!

Arctic fox

Fluffy Arctic foxes can change the color of their fur! They have a white coat that blends in with the snow in the winter, and a gray coat in summer.

Arctic tern

The Arctic tern goes on an incredible journey. Each year, it flies from the Arctic to the Antarctic and back again, covering thousands of miles.

South Pole

Emperor penguin

When it gets very cold, emperor penguins huddle together. These big birds can't fly, but they are excellent swimmers.

Bobtail squid

The amazing bobtail squid can glow in the dark! This neat trick helps it to blend in with bright water and hide from predators.

Polar bear

Polar bears might look cuddly, but they are fierce hunters. Their white coats help them to stay hidden in the snow.

North Pole

Narwhal

With their long, pointed tusks, narwhals have been called the unicorns of the sea.

Orca

These giant dolphins live in families called pods. They can swim while half-asleep! One side of their brain stays awake, while the other takes a nap.

Seal

Sleek seals can swim underwater, but live on the ice. They hunt fish in the deep water below.

Deep in the jungle

Tropical rainforests are made up of **four layers**. A mix of fascinating animals and plants lives in each one.

Monkey

Bat

Sloth

Parrot

Unusual animals

Because rainforests are warm, wet, and sheltered, lots of animals live here that can't be found anywhere else on Earth. How many animals can you spot in the trees?

Anteater

Bird

Butterfly

Snake

Layers of a rainforest

Emergent layer
Monkeys climb to the tops of tall trees, and birds fly up above.

Canopy
The canopy is a thick layer of treetops. It is home to animals such as bats and butterflies, and lots of climbing plants.

Understory
Shorter trees crowd here, such as palms, vines, and creepers. You'll find sloths, jaguars, snakes, and frogs enjoying the shady conditions under the canopy.

Forest floor
Down on the ground it's muddy and covered in leaves. It's the darkest part of the jungle and is home to lots of creepy-crawlies, such as ants, beetles, and millipedes.

127

Grassland animals

Are you ready to go on a trip through the **savanna**? What animals can you see **eating**, **hiding**, **and hunting** in the grassy landscape?

Prairie dog

This animal isn't a dog at all! It's actually a type of squirrel that lives in underground burrows.

Quokka

These furry little creatures hop around to find food. They also poke out their tongues to keep cool.

Zebra

No two zebras are the same. Each one has its own unique striped pattern.

What's for dinner?

Animals have different eating habits. Some hunt their food, others eat dead animals they find, and some graze on grasses and plants.

Elephants

Elephants munch on huge amounts of grass and leaves. Their poop, or dung, helps keep the soil healthy for more plants to grow.

Acacia trees

Few trees grow in grasslands, but you might spot a lone acacia tree in the distance.

Giraffe

Giraffes make use of their long necks to reach fresh, tasty leaves from treetops.

Emu

This tall bird walks for miles to find food. It feeds on plants and insects.

Vervet monkeys

Clever vervet monkeys live in big groups and often groom each other.

Dung beetle

These strong insects roll up big balls of animal poop to lay their eggs on. Stinky!

Lions

Big cats, such as lions, make excellent hunters. This is because they are fast and powerful and can hide in the grass.

Vultures

Vultures are scavengers. This means they feed on dead animals. They find these animals using their excellent eyesight and sense of smell.

129

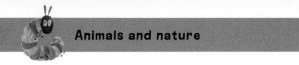
Hide and seek

Some animals' **coloring** or **pattern** allows them
to blend in with their surroundings. This is called
camouflage. It helps them to hide from other animals.

**How many chameleons
can you spot?**

Changing color

Some animals, such as chameleons,
can change color to match their
surroundings. They also change
color to stay cool or to show
that they're angry.

Dressing up

Some crabs decorate themselves by attaching tiny pieces of coral to their shells. The hermit crab protects its soft body by hiding inside an empty shell. It pokes its legs out to walk, taking its home around with it.

Changing coat

The Arctic hare's white fur blends in with the snow and ice in the winter. During the summer, its coat changes to brown, which makes the hare harder to spot against the ground and rocks.

Blending in

With their striped black-and-orange coats, tigers blend in with long grass and forests. Their camouflage keeps them hidden when they are sneaking up on prey.

Night creatures

When you go to bed, some animals **wake up**, ready for a busy night. They are called **nocturnal** animals. Large ears and big eyes help them find things to eat in the darkness.

Wolf

Wolves are found in many colder countries, living in family groups called packs. They work together to hunt for food.

Raccoon

In North America, Europe, and Japan, raccoons use their paws to feel around for food and their strong noses to sniff out what's nearby.

Bush baby

These African creatures dart through trees and across the ground in search of insects to eat.

Owl

Found all around the world, owls have excellent hearing. From high in the sky, they pick up the noises of things scurrying below.

Fireflies

These insects glow in the dark in many parts of the world. Their light attracts mates—and in some cases, other fireflies to eat!

Bat

Bats fly through the dark skies of many countries. They make sounds that bounce off moths and other prey. This tells the bat where the prey is. This special skill is called echolocation.

Hedgehog

Snuffling through the undergrowth in Europe, Asia, and New Zealand, hedgehogs sniff out creepy-crawlies.

Super senses

You might not be able to see in the dark, but many nocturnal animals can! Some also have superb hearing to figure out what's around them, or a strong sense of touch.

5. Chicken

4. Chick

1. Egg

2. Egg hatching

3. Hatchling

Chicken

A mother chicken lays eggs in a nest. She keeps them nice and warm by sitting on them. When the chicks are strong enough, they hatch from their shells. They have fluffy feathers that are replaced with stiffer, darker ones as they grow.

3. Chrysalis

The caterpillar wraps itself up in a hard case called a chrysalis. It is while hiding in here that the caterpillar undergoes an amazing transformation.

Life cycles

The **different stages** an animal goes through are called its **life cycle**. Some animals are born in **eggs**, then when the females are fully grown, they lay their own eggs, so the cycle can begin again.

Butterfly

Would you guess that a little egg lying on a leaf could turn into a beautiful butterfly? Butterflies look completely different at each stage of their life cycle.

4. Butterfly

A beautiful butterfly emerges from the chrysalis, ready to lay eggs all over again.

1. Egg

A butterfly lays an egg on a leaf.

2. Caterpillar

A little caterpillar hatches from the egg. It is very hungry, so munches away on leaves, getting bigger and bigger.

5. Adult frog

4. Froglet

1. Eggs

3. Developing legs

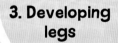

2. Tadpole

Frog

Frogs are amphibians, which means they can live on land and in water. They start their lives as eggs in water, then hatch into swimming tadpoles, before growing into jumping frogs.

History

A trip to the museum

Visiting a museum is like taking a journey through time to **learn about history**. What shall we look at first?

Dinosaur fossils, like this Tyrannosaurus skeleton, have been carefully pieced together like puzzles for you to see in museums. They are millions of years old!

Dinosaurs

Prehistoric peoples
Early humans made tools for hunting animals. They created sharp arrow points out of bone or stone.

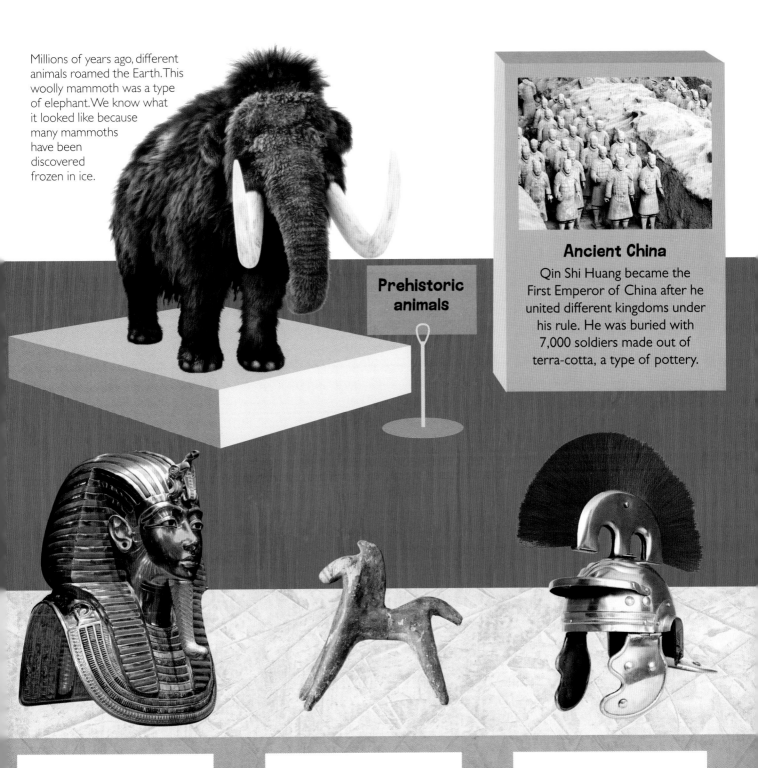

Millions of years ago, different animals roamed the Earth. This woolly mammoth was a type of elephant. We know what it looked like because many mammoths have been discovered frozen in ice.

Prehistoric animals

Ancient China
Qin Shi Huang became the First Emperor of China after he united different kingdoms under his rule. He was buried with 7,000 soldiers made out of terra-cotta, a type of pottery.

Ancient Egypt
The ancient Egyptian king Tutankhamun had a gold death mask made for his burial. It's more than 3,000 years old and very heavy.

Ancient Greece
Gods were very important to the people of ancient Greece. This terra-cotta horse was a gift for the gods.

Ancient Rome
More than 2,000 years ago, the Roman army ruled over many countries. The soldiers wore helmets topped with horsehair.

Dinosaurs

Millions of years ago, strange **reptiles** called **dinosaurs** walked the Earth. Some were the size of chickens, but others would have towered over you.

Diplodocus
Dinosaurs with long necks, such as Diplodocus, are called sauropods.

What are dinosaurs?

Reptiles that lived from around 230 million years ago to 66 million years ago are called dinosaurs. Some ate meat (carnivores), while others munched on leaves (herbivores), and they walked on two or four legs.

Tyrannosaurus
The fearsome Tyrannosaurus had huge, sharp teeth—perfect for eating its prey!

Pterodactylus

This flying reptile wasn't a dinosaur, but lived at the same time.

Birds

After a huge asteroid hit Earth, all the dinosaurs died... except birds! They still live with us today.

Feathered or not

For a long time, people thought that all dinosaurs had scales, like modern reptiles. However, some had colorful feathers covering their bodies.

Triceratops

This leaf-eater had three horns and a bony frill to protect itself from predators.

Stegosaurus

Bony plates along its back helped Stegosaurus attract a mate.

Ferocious fossils

We know that dinosaurs existed because of traces they left behind in rock, called fossils. Here are two common types.

Footprints

Dinosaurs left footprints in mud that turned into rock over millions of years.

Poop

Some dinosaur poop can be seen in ancient rock! This can tell us what a dinosaur ate.

Bow and arrow

Hunting
Stone Age people hunted animals with sharpened sticks, spears, or bows and arrows. They also gathered fruits and nuts to eat.

Prehistoric peoples

Early humans lived in huts or caves and used **tools** made from stone. This time was called the **Stone Age**. It began about 3.3 million years ago and ended about 4,000 years ago, when people had learned to farm.

Spear

Falcon

Making fire

Early humans learned to make fire about 1.5 million years ago. Fire gave them warmth and light, and it was also used for cooking.

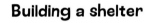

Building a shelter

To shelter from the weather, early humans learned to build huts using wooden poles. These were covered in animal skins and tree bark.

Ancient Egypt

Ancient Egypt, in **northeastern Africa**, was one of the **earliest civilizations**, lasting from 3100 BCE to 30 BCE. It had kings and queens, incredible buildings, and many interesting traditions.

Pyramids

The pyramids were built 4,500 years ago as burial places for powerful pharaohs. They were filled with treasure, paintings, and carvings.

Cobra

The symbol of the goddess Wadjet featured an Egyptian cobra standing up. This poisonous snake was a symbol of royalty.

Cats

Cats were considered good luck by ancient Egyptians. Most families kept them as pets, with some even dressing them in jewelry.

Mummies

When important ancient Egyptians died, their bodies were specially prepared for the afterlife. Their organs were removed and the bodies were wrapped up tightly with cloths.

A mummy was buried in a coffin called a sarcophagus.

The Nile River ran through the heart of ancient Egypt.

Farming

Ancient Egyptian farmers grew vegetables and crops. Cows were very helpful on farms for pulling plows and for providing milk and meat.

Beetles

A type of insect called a scarab beetle was a symbol of the god of the sun, Khepri.

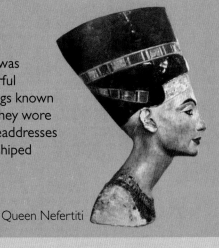

Pharaohs

Ancient Egypt was ruled by powerful queens and kings known as pharaohs. They wore special royal headdresses and were worshiped like gods.

Queen Nefertiti

Hieroglyphs

Picture symbols called hieroglyphs were used for writing. Scribes were important people who learned to read and write for their job.

The Parthenon in Athens, Greece

Greek vase

Ancient Greece

The ancient Greeks lived from about 1200 BCE to 600 CE. They are famous for their **art**, **buildings**, and **plays**.

Gods and goddesses

Many people in ancient Greece believed that there were lots of gods and goddesses who were responsible for different things, such as war, love, and the afterlife.

Zeus Aphrodite Apollo Hades

The Colosseum in Rome, Italy

Ancient Rome

The ancient Romans ruled a **large empire** about 2,000 years ago. Its capital city was **Rome**, in modern-day Italy.

Roman soldiers

These fearsome warriors were well trained and wore armor made from metal links called chain mail.

Roman society

There were many people who lived in ancient Rome. They were split into different groups, depending on what they did in Roman society.

Emperor **Citizen** **Freedwoman** **Slave**

147

China through time

China has had a huge impact on the world with famous **inventions**, such as silk and paper. **Art**, especially pottery and painting, is also a large part of Chinese culture.

The first emperor of China united several kingdoms into one in 221 BCE.

The Great Wall

The Great Wall of China was begun over 2,000 years ago. It is 5,500 miles (8,850 km) long.

Terra-cotta Army

An army of statues was built by 700,000 workers to guard the tomb of the first emperor, Qin Shi Huang.

Porcelain

Chinese porcelain, a type of pottery, is very valuable. It is often decorated with beautiful pictures and paintings.

Chinese dragons

Chinese dragons are legendary creatures made up of parts of many other animals. They are said to be kind and caring, but also represent power and strength.

Writing

Early Chinese writing developed from drawing pictures of objects. Today, people use around 3,500 different characters.

右二冊廿葉章侯妙蹟余兄
王甫公所愛護同治甲戌畀子
藏之廿餘年来職事倥偬
不遑展覷光緒六月客有劄
老蓮白門剪兩圖並神女巨
軸其高尋支涸海內奇蹟回出
冊相与歡賞客退獨坐擔然
回憶柏古軒中鬻茗燕香品
評讀畫香如隔世日月迥邁

Silk

The Chinese made silk from silkworm cocoons around 5,500 years ago. China kept the secret of how to make silk for over a thousand years.

All about castles

Did you know there are castles all around the **world**? These strong structures were built to **protect** kings, queens, and other important people from their **enemies**.

Castle design

Castles were often built on hills so they were difficult to reach. Sometimes they had small towns around them.

Flag
Every castle had its own flag, called a standard.

The walkway on top of a tower is called a battlement.

Most castles had thick stone walls.

Some castles had a water-filled ditch, or moat, for extra protection.

A drawbridge lifted up to keep enemies out.

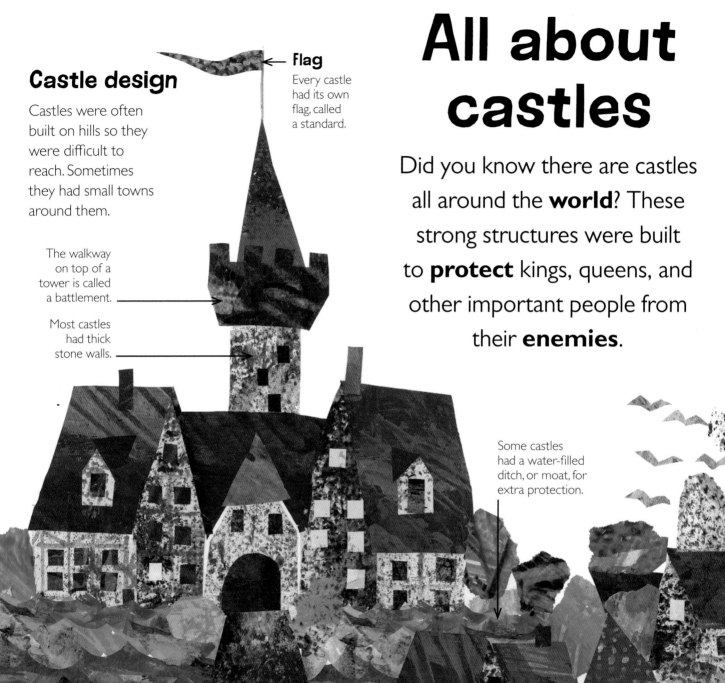

Jousting

In the Middle Ages, knights took part in tournaments to entertain crowds. They mounted horses and charged toward each other while carrying long poles. The goal was to knock their opponent off their horse!

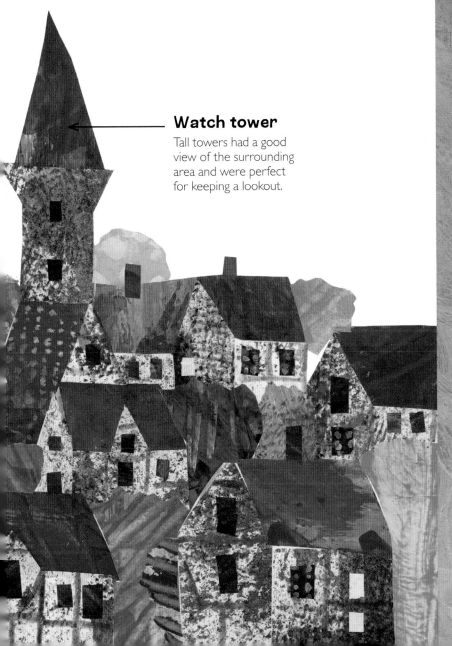

Watch tower
Tall towers had a good view of the surrounding area and were perfect for keeping a lookout.

Castles today

Castles come in many shapes and sizes. Here are some styles from around the world.

Marksburg Castle
Soaring high above the Rhine River in Germany, this impressive castle has seen many battles but never been destroyed.

Himeji Castle
This beautiful Japanese castle has survived wars and earthquakes. One bomb even hit the roof, but, luckily, it didn't explode!

Krak des Chevaliers
Two rings of thick wall kept attackers out of this castle in Syria. It was big enough to protect around 2,000 people!

Exploring the world

Throughout history, people have made **journeys** to **explore** the many mountains, oceans, and continents on **our planet**.

The compass was invented in China and first used for ships to find their way. It uses a magnetic needle that always points north.

Explorers

Between the 10th and 18th centuries, many European explorers took to the seas and claimed to discover new lands. Most of these places actually already had people living there.

Shipwrecks

Deep down on the seabed, you can find the sunken remains of ships. People have found treasure such as silver, gold, and jewels inside some of these unlucky boats.

Scuba divers can explore underwater for a long time by taking tanks filled with air.

Extreme adventures

Some adventurers dare to explore the most extreme places on Earth. They might climb high mountains, cross cold continents, or dive deep into the sea.

Discovery

By traveling, explorers can find interesting things. Plants and animals are different around the world, and there is still a lot to learn about our planet.

Once upon a time...

Throughout history, people have always told **stories**. Some stories are funny, while others help us learn things. Here are some **traditional tales** from around the world.

The Thirsty Frog

The First Australians have a strong history of sharing stories, often about nature. One tale they retell is about Tiddalik, a thirsty frog who drinks all the water in the land and has to learn to share.

Arabian Nights

Aladdin is one of the stories from the *Arabian Nights* collection. These exciting tales often feature magic and adventure. They were first told by market storytellers in the Middle East and began to be written down around the 9th century.

The Little Mermaid

This story was written by Danish author Hans Christian Andersen in 1837. It tells the story of a mermaid who wants to become human. Have you heard of this tale?

Anansi

The tales of Anansi the trickster spider originated in Ghana, West Africa. These stories often teach people about right and wrong.

Story time

Many fairy tales, legends, and myths feature similar characters, themes, and settings. Can you make up a story using some of the things below?

Castle

Ghost

Magic

Pirate ship

Royalty

Monster

Dragon

Giant

Wolf

Fairy

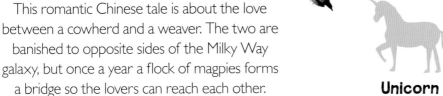

The Cowherd and the Weaver Girl

This romantic Chinese tale is about the love between a cowherd and a weaver. The two are banished to opposite sides of the Milky Way galaxy, but once a year a flock of magpies forms a bridge so the lovers can reach each other.

Unicorn

Genie

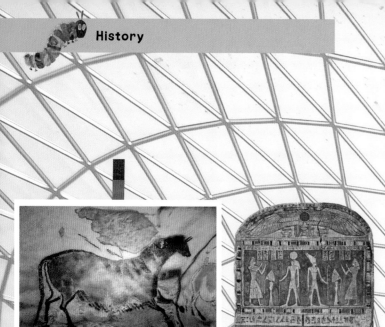

Cave art
The earliest known cave painting is from 45,000 years ago. The artists used natural materials, such as charcoal.

Egyptian painting
Some Ancient Egyptian artists painted pictures of their gods and leaders on pieces of wood.

Chinese porcelain
Delicate, painted porcelain pottery was first made in China over 2,000 years ago.

Classical sculptures
Lifelike sculptures of people were made in ancient Greece and Rome.

A history of art

People have always loved **being creative**. We have found **paintings** on cave walls made thousands of years ago. You can discover lots of types of art in all colors, shapes, and sizes by visiting an **art gallery**.

Renaissance

From the 1300s to the 1600s, artists painted magnificent pictures. They often copied classical art.

Impressionism

People tried to show more light and movement in their paintings in the 1800s. Many used dabs of paint to do this.

Abstract

In abstract art, paintings or sculptures don't need to be lifelike at all! They might show a mood instead.

Eric Carle

Beautiful art can make great stories even better! Eric Carle has illustrated more than 70 books, with stories about animals big and small, nature, hope, love, and more. Eric Carle's illustrations are featured in this book! Can you find any on this page?

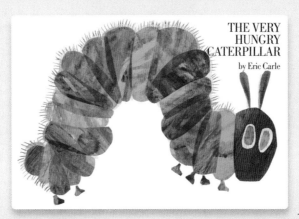

The Very Hungry Caterpillar was first published in 1969, with holes in the pages to show the caterpillar eating through many different foods.

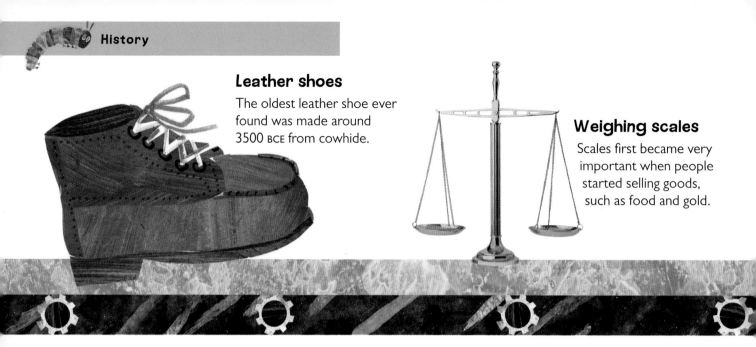

Leather shoes
The oldest leather shoe ever found was made around 3500 BCE from cowhide.

Weighing scales
Scales first became very important when people started selling goods, such as food and gold.

Incredible inventions

An invention is something that has never been made before. It might **solve a problem** or **make life easier** in some way. Here are some of the most important inventions in history.

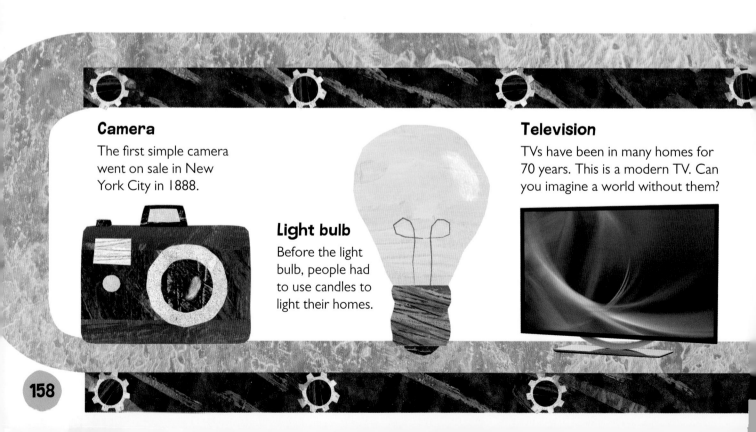

Camera
The first simple camera went on sale in New York City in 1888.

Light bulb
Before the light bulb, people had to use candles to light their homes.

Television
TVs have been in many homes for 70 years. This is a modern TV. Can you imagine a world without them?

Paper

In 100 CE in China, a man named Cai Lun first created paper from plant fibers.

Abacus

The abacus was the first type of calculator. It was invented around 190 CE in China. This is a colorful, modern abacus.

Telephone

The telephone was invented in 1876. Phones did not always look like the ones we see today.

Square-bottomed paper bag

American inventor Margaret Knight began inventing as a child. Later, she designed a machine to fold paper bags.

Printing press

The printing press, first built around 1440, helps us to make magazines and books.

Antibiotics

The first antibiotic, used to treat infections, was discovered in Britain in the 1920s.

Ballpoint pen

Before the ballpoint pen was created in 1945, fountain pens used to leak messy ink.

Smartphone

Smartphones can connect to the internet, which allows us to share information easily. The first one was invented in 1992.

Transportation

Thousands of years ago, most people rarely traveled far from home, and they often went by foot. Modern transportation now takes us many places, **by land**, **by water**, and **by air**.

Sailing ships

In ancient Greece and ancient Egypt, people first had the idea to add sails to ships. Wind blowing behind the sails makes a vessel go much faster.

Steam train

Steam trains were invented in the 19th century. Soon they were powerful enough to carry lots of goods and people.

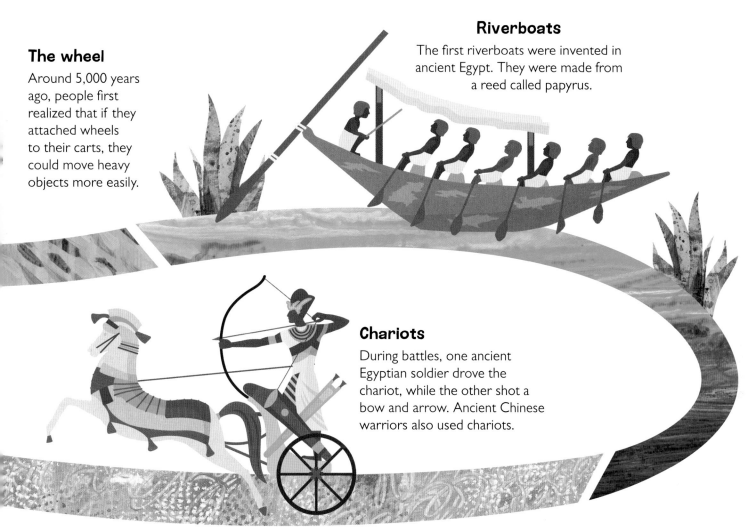

The wheel

Around 5,000 years ago, people first realized that if they attached wheels to their carts, they could move heavy objects more easily.

Riverboats

The first riverboats were invented in ancient Egypt. They were made from a reed called papyrus.

Chariots

During battles, one ancient Egyptian soldier drove the chariot, while the other shot a bow and arrow. Ancient Chinese warriors also used chariots.

High-wheeler

The high-wheeler, with its enormous front wheel, was one of the first bicycles. It was invented in 1871.

Car

In 1894, the German Benz factory built the first car powered by a gas engine. It looked like a huge tricycle!

The Wright Flyer

In 1903, the Wright brothers made the first successful powered flight in the world. The plane stayed in the air for 12 seconds.

Terrific toys

Children have played with toys for thousands of years. Some **early toys**, such as balls, blocks, or board games, haven't changed all that much. Let's **play**!

Dominoes

This game of matching the ends of pieces comes from China. It is played all over the world.

Modeling clay

Modeling clay was first used as wallpaper cleaner! It's now a fun way to create models.

Teddy bear

These cuddly toys were first created in Germany about 100 years ago.

The oldest toy in the world is a baby's rattle found in Turkey. It is around 4,000 years old!

Ludo

Ludo is similar to the Indian board game Pachisi, which was created in the 6th century. The goal is for players to get all their pieces around the board.

Jump rope

Jump ropes have a long history. They are used in jumping games in China and were used by ancient Egyptian athletes.

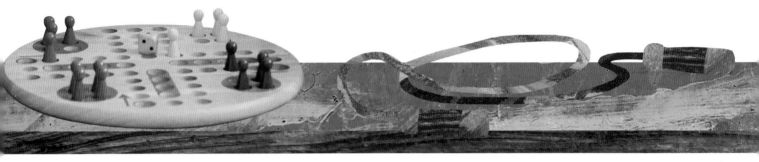

Egyptian balls

These ancient toys are made of fabric and plants. They have small stones that rattle inside them.

Slinky

This coiled spring can walk down stairs by itself. It was invented by mistake and first intended to be used at sea.

Building blocks

Blocks have been popular toys for hundreds of years. It's fun to build tall towers with them!

Yo-yo

This ancient spinning toy was first created in China. You can impress your friends by learning to do tricks with it.

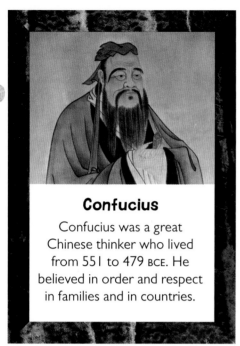

Confucius

Confucius was a great Chinese thinker who lived from 551 to 479 BCE. He believed in order and respect in families and in countries.

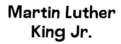

Martin Luther King Jr.

In the 1950s and 1960s, Martin Luther King Jr. led the campaign for equal rights for Black Americans in the United States.

History's heroes

Many amazing people helped to shape the world we live in today, from **inventors** and **scientists** to **artists** and **writers**. How would you like to change the world?

Marie Curie

Marie Curie was a scientist whose work led to better treatments for a common illness called cancer.

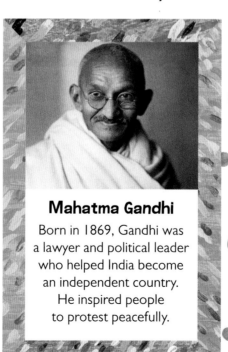

Mahatma Gandhi

Born in 1869, Gandhi was a lawyer and political leader who helped India become an independent country. He inspired people to protest peacefully.

Isaac Newton

An English scientist, Isaac Newton is famous for describing how gravity works after noticing an apple falling from a tree.

Ada Lovelace

A British mathematician, Ada Lovelace was the first computer programmer. She worked on programs for early forms of the computer.

Katsushika Hokusai

Katsushika Hokusai was a Japanese artist. His most famous work was the *Great Wave* print, which he made by carving a picture into a woodblock.

Amelia Earhart

An American pilot, Amelia Earhart was the first woman to fly solo across the Atlantic Ocean in 1932.

Katherine Johnson

Mathematician Katherine Johnson worked at NASA. Her calculations made many space missions possible, including Apollo 11.

William Shakespeare

One of the world's greatest playwrights, Shakespeare was born in 1564. His plays, such as *Romeo and Juliet* and *Hamlet*, are still performed all over the world.

Science, math, and technology

States of matter

The materials that make up the world around us come in **three different forms**: solid, liquid, and gas. These are called **states of matter**. All matter is made up of **particles**— tiny parts that are too small to see.

Solid

Solids are materials that keep their shape. They are usually hard, such as a metal car. Solids are made up of particles that are close together and fixed in shape.

Robot

Broccoli

Car

Liquid

Liquids, such as water and paint, change shape to fit the container they're in. They flow and can be poured. Liquids are made of particles that sit slightly apart and can move around.

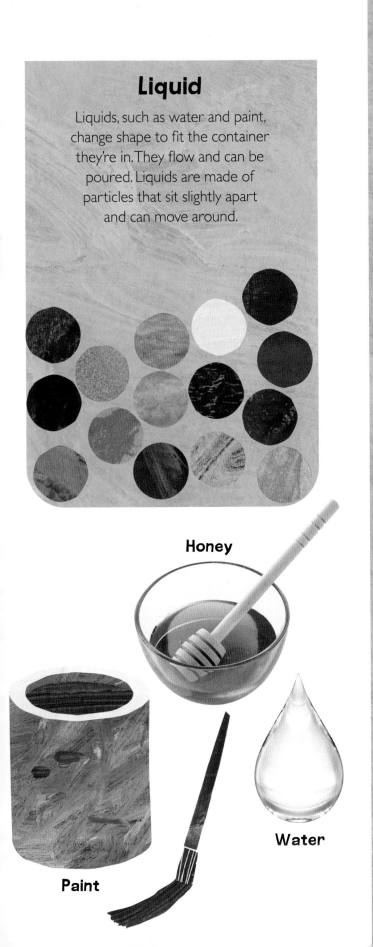

Honey

Paint

Water

Gas

Most gases, such as air, are invisible. They can fit into a small space, such as a balloon, or spread out to fill a large space, such as a room. Their particles can move quickly and freely.

Balloons

Pool ring

Bubbles

Materials

Materials are marvelous! Every object on Earth is made of a material. Some, such as fabric, are **soft** and **flexible**. Others, such as bricks, are **hard** and **strong**.

Glass

This hard material is transparent, or see-through. It has many uses. It can be used to make things such as windows, eyeglasses, and drinking glasses.

You can clearly see the orange juice in this drinking glass.

Fabric

Soft fabric is easy to cut and sew. It's made of threads that come from lots of different places, such as plants, animals, and plastic.

This pencil case is made from fabric threads woven together.

Plastic

Plastic can be either hard or soft. It is very easy to shape and does not break easily. Plastic isn't found in nature—we make it from chemicals.

The outside of this pen is made from shiny plastic.

Properties

All materials have different properties. This means they look, feel, and act differently. Sponges, for example, are absorbent, which means they can hold water. Can you name these materials?

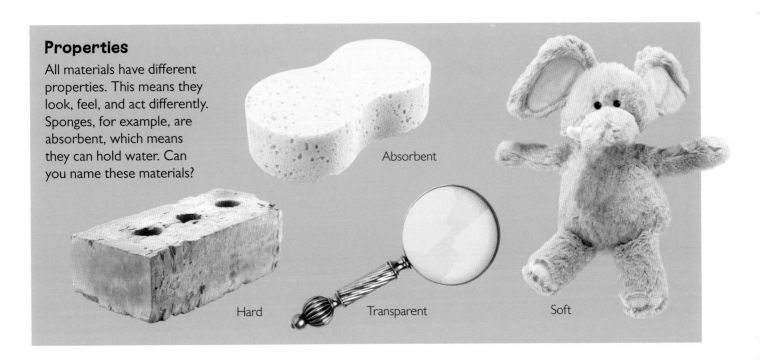

Absorbent

Hard

Transparent

Soft

Metal

There are many different types of metal. Most are strong and can be hammered into different shapes without breaking. Some metals are magnetic, which means that they are attracted to magnets.

Most paper clips are made from a metal called steel.

Wood

This strong material comes from trees. It does not break easily, so it can be used to make many things, such as furniture, musical instruments, and pencils.

Paper is very thin, light, and easy to mark.

Paper

Paper is made by mixing small pieces of wood with water. Some types of paper, such as cardboard, are stronger than others, such as tissue paper.

Pencils are made from an outer shell of wood.

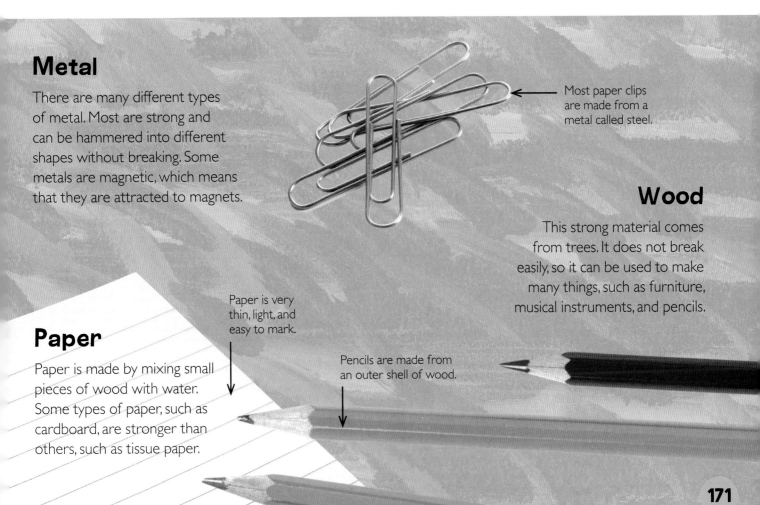

Colors

Can you imagine the world without color? It would be a very boring place. **Colorful things are all around us**—from clothes and toys to nature and art.

Yellow

Yellow is the color of sunshine, lemons, and sunflowers. What other yellow things can you think of?

Orange

Oranges are orange. This bright color is also the color of goldfish, fall leaves, and pumpkins.

Red

In addition to being the color of sweet strawberries and crunchy apples, red is also a warning color. The red traffic light tells you to stop.

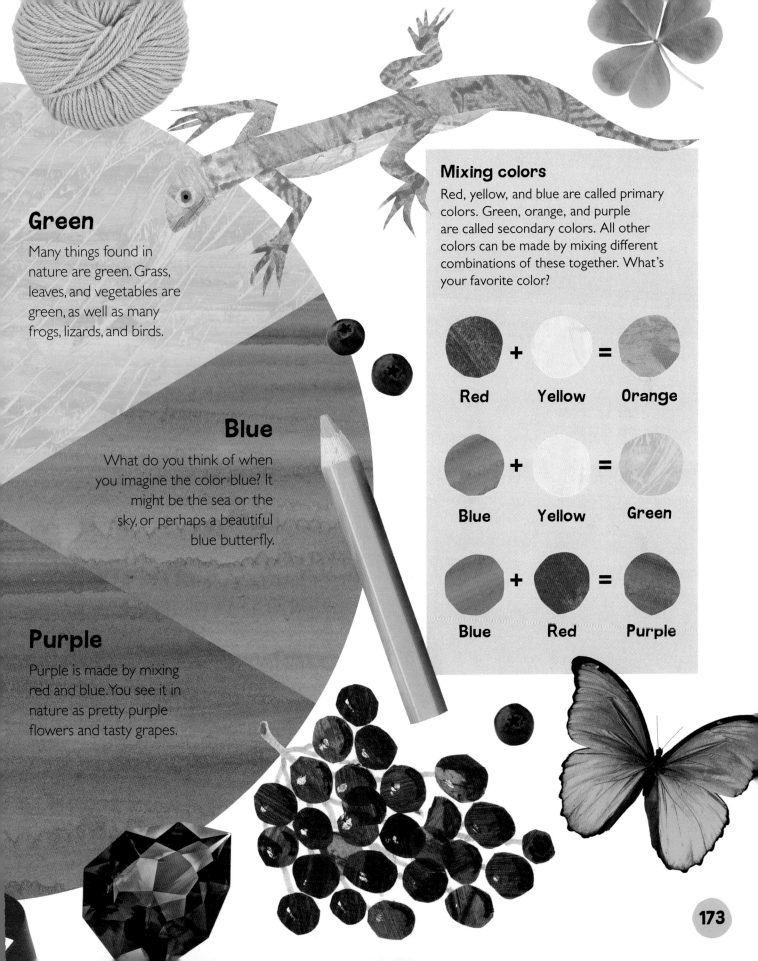

Green

Many things found in nature are green. Grass, leaves, and vegetables are green, as well as many frogs, lizards, and birds.

Blue

What do you think of when you imagine the color blue? It might be the sea or the sky, or perhaps a beautiful blue butterfly.

Purple

Purple is made by mixing red and blue. You see it in nature as pretty purple flowers and tasty grapes.

Mixing colors

Red, yellow, and blue are called primary colors. Green, orange, and purple are called secondary colors. All other colors can be made by mixing different combinations of these together. What's your favorite color?

Red + Yellow = Orange

Blue + Yellow = Green

Blue + Red = Purple

Light

Light is a form of **energy** that we can see.
All living things on planet Earth need light.
It keeps us warm, helps our food grow,
and allows us to **see things**.

Splitting light

Light that we can see is called white light, but it's actually made up of seven colors. It can be split into colors by shining it through a triangular block of glass called a prism.

Sunbeam
A beam of light shines onto the prism.

Prism

Light bends
When light passes through a prism, it slows down and bends.

Rainbow colors
The light splits into separate colors. How many colors can you see?

Light travels faster than anything else.

Making rainbows

When sunlight passes through raindrops, it makes a rainbow. The raindrops act like tiny prisms, splitting the light into different colors.

Without light, you wouldn't be able to see anything.

Shadows

A shadow is made when an object blocks the sun. The size and shape depends on where the sun is in the sky.

Sun is high

In the middle of the day, the sun is high in the sky and the cat has a short shadow.

Sun is behind

When the sun is behind the cat, its shadow is in front.

Sun is low

In the morning or the evening, the sun is low and the cat has a long shadow.

When a sound travels through the
air, it squeezes and stretches the
air in invisible sound waves.

Sound

A bell **ringing**. A dog **barking**. A
car **honking**. Sounds are all around us.
All sounds start with a **vibration**. These
vibrations travel through the air, and when
they reach your ear, you hear the sound.

Volume

Can you think of some soft
sounds and some loud sounds?
Loud sounds have bigger sound
waves. A sound's loudness,
or volume, is measured in
decibels. More decibels
means louder sound.

Roarrrrr!

Quiet sound

Falling leaves
A leaf falling is almost impossible to hear! It makes a sound of only 10 decibels.

Getting louder

Roaring tiger
A tiger's roar can measure 114 decibels, if you are standing nearby! It is 25 times louder than a lawn mower.

Really LOUD!

Launching Rocket
When a rocket launches, it can reach 180 decibels. The spacecraft must be very strong so that the vibrations do not damage it.

Fun forces

Whether you're **zooming** down a slide or **bouncing** on a seesaw, forces are at play. A force can either be a **push** or a **pull**, affecting how objects move.

Push forward

The harder the push, the higher you swing!

Push up

These children are using force from their legs to push up from the ground.

Friction

This force slows the child's movement down the slide. Bumpy surfaces have a lot of friction, but smooth surfaces have less.

Gravity

An invisible force called gravity pulls everything and everyone down toward the ground.

Balanced forces

When forces are used equally in opposite directions, they balance. The forces cancel each other out, so the rope does not move in either direction.

Pull

Both the dog and the child are pulling on the dog's leash in different directions.

3, 2, 1... GO!

Everything **moves** at its own **speed**. The **faster** an object is going, the more speed it has. What's the fastest thing you can think of?

Koalas can run very fast, but they prefer to spend their time resting in trees!

A snail moves slowly, pushing itself along with one squishy, long muscle.

The wheels of a skateboard are smooth, which helps them go around faster.

Athlete

People who train to run fast are called sprinters. They have to work hard to build up their muscles.

Cockroach

These insects can scuttle around very quickly. They are fastest when they rear up onto their two back legs.

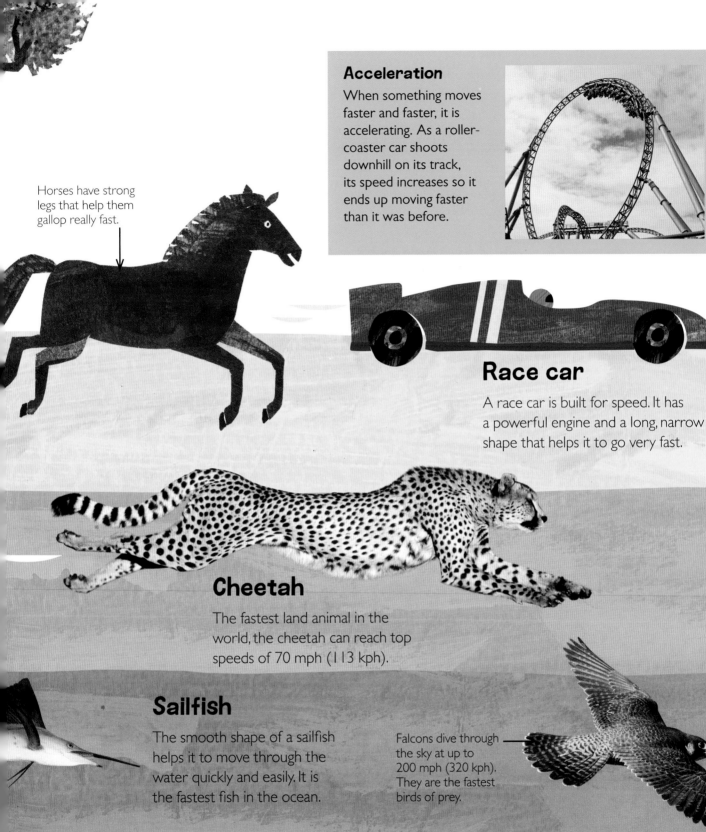

Acceleration

When something moves faster and faster, it is accelerating. As a roller-coaster car shoots downhill on its track, its speed increases so it ends up moving faster than it was before.

Horses have strong legs that help them gallop really fast.

Race car

A race car is built for speed. It has a powerful engine and a long, narrow shape that helps it to go very fast.

Cheetah

The fastest land animal in the world, the cheetah can reach top speeds of 70 mph (113 kph).

Sailfish

The smooth shape of a sailfish helps it to move through the water quickly and easily. It is the fastest fish in the ocean.

Falcons dive through the sky at up to 200 mph (320 kph). They are the fastest birds of prey.

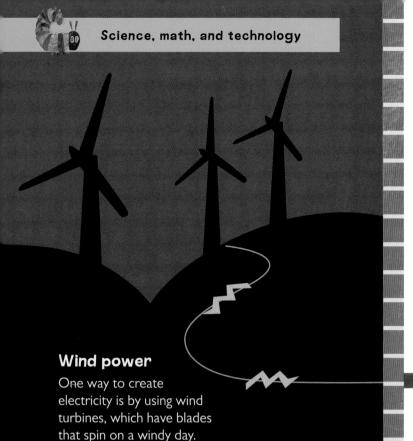

Circuit

Electricity is needed to power objects, such as a light bulb. Electricity reaches the light bulb by flowing through a loop called a circuit.

When the switch is turned on, the light bulb turns on, too.

Wind power

One way to create electricity is by using wind turbines, which have blades that spin on a windy day. These power a generator that produces electricity.

Electricity

What **powers** your toaster so it can make a yummy snack? The answer is a type of **energy** called electricity. It can be created, or **generated**, in different ways, and is very useful in everyday life.

Always be extra careful when using electrical objects.

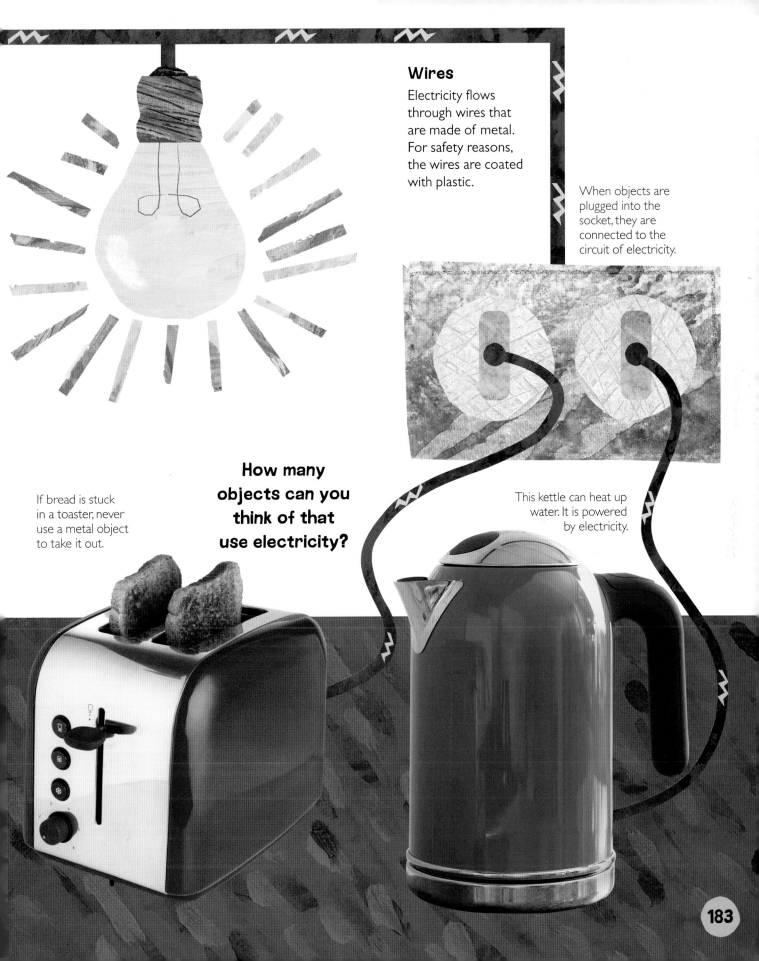

Wires

Electricity flows through wires that are made of metal. For safety reasons, the wires are coated with plastic.

When objects are plugged into the socket, they are connected to the circuit of electricity.

How many objects can you think of that use electricity?

If bread is stuck in a toaster, never use a metal object to take it out.

This kettle can heat up water. It is powered by electricity.

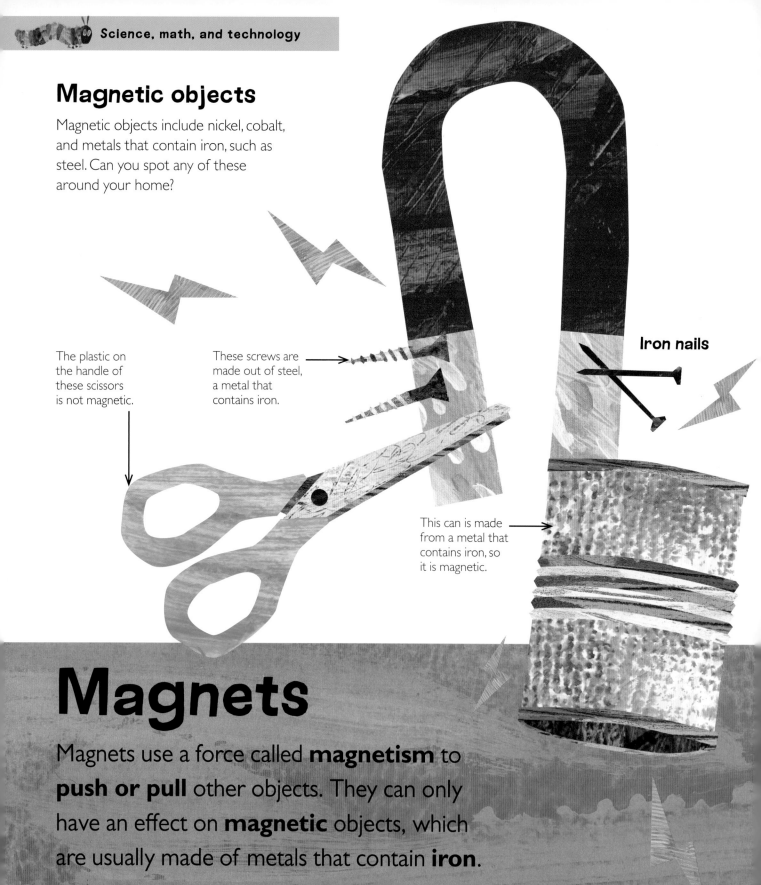

Magnetic objects

Magnetic objects include nickel, cobalt, and metals that contain iron, such as steel. Can you spot any of these around your home?

The plastic on the handle of these scissors is not magnetic.

These screws are made out of steel, a metal that contains iron.

Iron nails

This can is made from a metal that contains iron, so it is magnetic.

Magnets

Magnets use a force called **magnetism** to **push or pull** other objects. They can only have an effect on **magnetic** objects, which are usually made of metals that contain **iron**.

Nonmagnetic objects

Any objects that do not contain iron or other magnetic materials are not magnetic. For example, metals like gold and materials like glass. This means that they will be unaffected by a magnet. Is a T-shirt magnetic?

Flowers

Glass vase

This apple is not made out of iron, so it is not affected by the magnet.

This book is made out of paper, which is not a magnetic material.

Crayons

Magnetic poles

On all magnets, the force of magnetism is strongest at the ends, called poles. Straight bar magnets have a north pole at one end and a south pole at the other. See how they affect each other!

The same poles repel—or push away—each other.

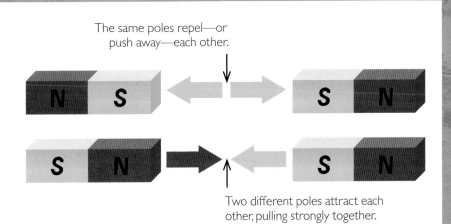

N S   S N

S N   S N

Two different poles attract each other, pulling strongly together.

Positions

In front and behind, left and right—these useful words all describe the **position of something**. Look at the pictures. Which ones show over and under? How about near and far?

Right

Left

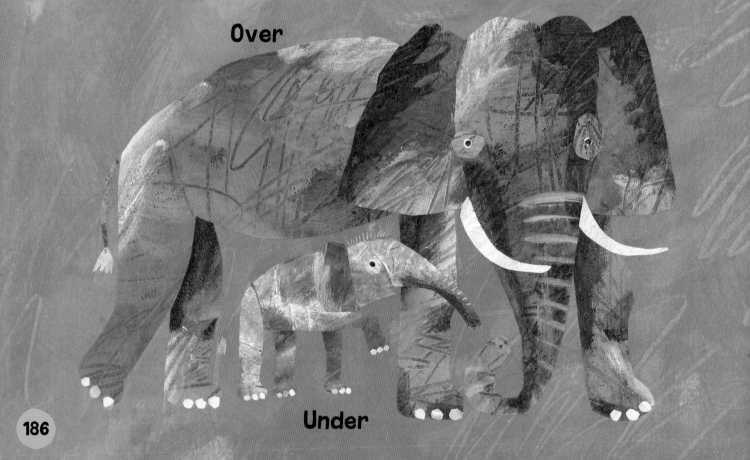

Over

Under

Behind

In front

In

Out

In-between

Beside

Far

Near

Together

187

Clever computers

Computers are amazing. They work by following simple **instructions**, or **codes**. Let's learn to think like a computer!

Following instructions

Coding means telling a computer what to do. To write a code, you need to give the computer simple instructions to follow. This is similar to giving recipe instructions or directions.

Crawl forward

Turn right

Turn left

Code the caterpillar!

Can you use these instructions to guide the caterpillar to the apple? Try to avoid the animals hiding in the maze!

Start

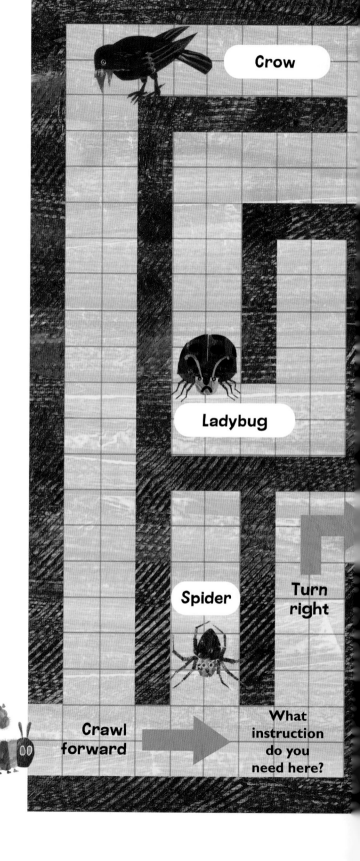

Crow

Ladybug

Spider

Turn right

Crawl forward

What instruction do you need here?

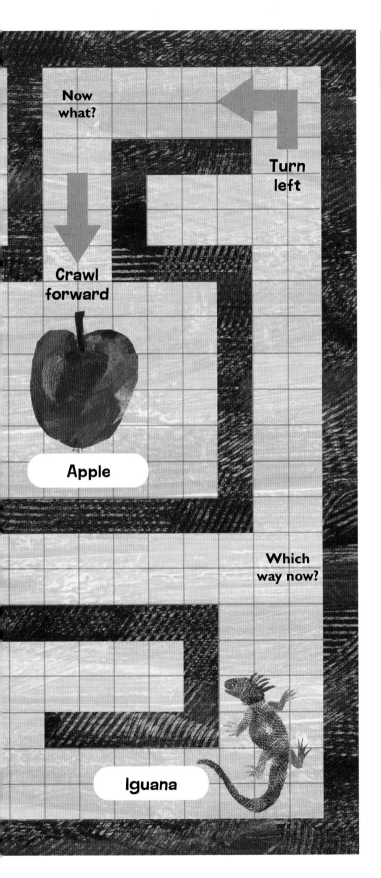

Now what?

Turn left

Crawl forward

Apple

Which way now?

Iguana

Computers

Computers are machines that store information and perform tasks. They've changed and become more advanced over time. Some are very large, but others are small enough to fit on your wrist!

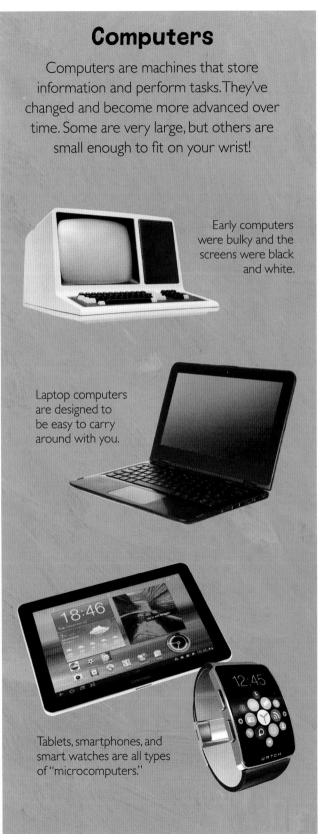

Early computers were bulky and the screens were black and white.

Laptop computers are designed to be easy to carry around with you.

Tablets, smartphones, and smart watches are all types of "microcomputers."

Numbers

Numbers can be used to explain lots of different things. They help us to tell the **time**, measure **sizes** and **distances**, and phone people.

When a number is less than zero, it is called a negative number and is shown with a minus symbol.

The number zero represents nothing. It is what is left when you eat everything on your plate!

Numbers everywhere

These mathematical symbols are all around us. We use numbers in everyday life, from doing addition to weighing food to knowing the speed limit on a road.

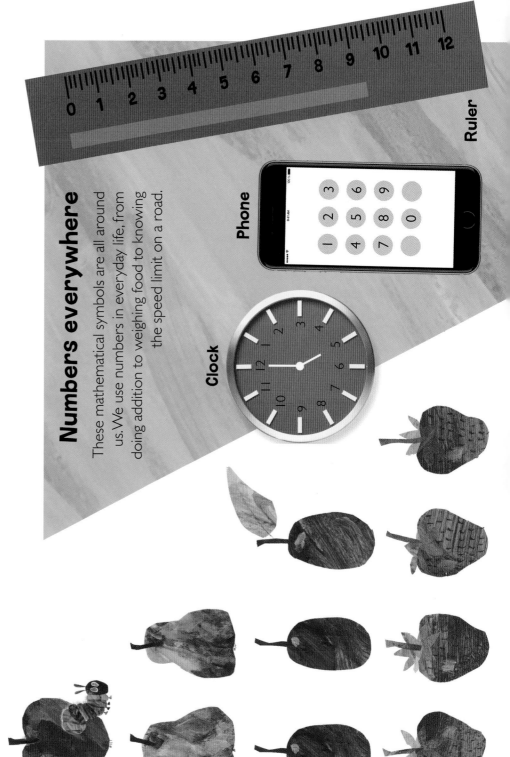

Ruler

Phone

Clock

-1

0

1

2

3

4

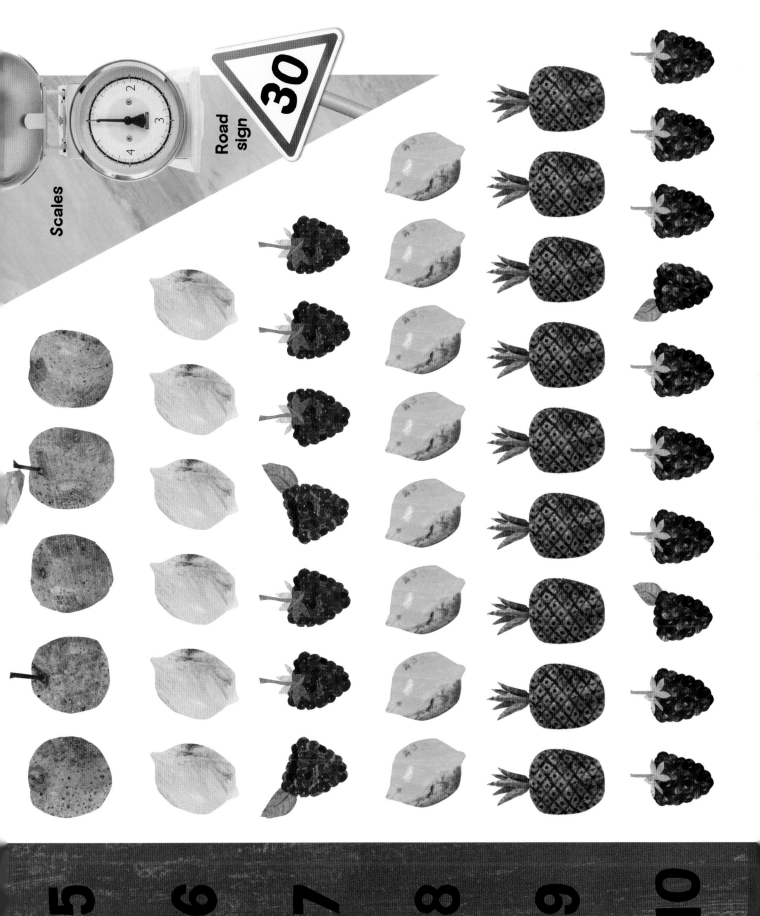

Scales

Road sign

30

5

6

7

8

9

10

My daily routine

Most of the time, we do similar things in a similar **order** every day. We wake up, have breakfast, then go to school. This is called our daily routine, and it helps us to **keep track** of things.

Sleeping
We spend most of the night snuggled up, fast asleep.

Bedtime
Shhh! It's nighttime now, so it's time for bed. Do you like to read a story before bed?

Nighttime

Evening

Bath time
It's good to have a bath or shower to get nice and clean before bed. Bath toys are optional!

Having dinner
You have dinner in the late afternoon or early evening. Yum, yum!

Wake up

Do you know what time you wake up? It's usually in the morning, soon after dawn, when the sun rises. After you jump out of bed, it's time to get dressed!

Breakfast

After you wake up and get dressed, it's breakfast time! It's key to have a healthy breakfast to get the day off to a good start.

Morning

School

Most children go to school each weekday morning. You often do things in a similar order each day, such as start with classes and then have playtime.

Afternoon

Eating lunch

Lunch is usually in the middle of the day. You might bring a packed lunch or have food made at the school. Then it's time for more learning!

Going home

Toward the end of the afternoon, it's time to go home. Do you walk, cycle, take the bus, or drive there?

Telling time

A clock tells us the time. The short hand on an analog clock points to the hours, and the long hand points to minutes. What time is this clock showing?

The long hand points to minutes.

The short hand points to hours.

These numbers show the 12 hours in each half of the day.

These lines show minutes.

Time

Time helps us to **organize our lives**. It tells us when to get up in the morning and even how old we are. We measure time in **seconds**, **minutes**, **hours**, **days**, **and years**.

Minutes and hours

Each day is divided into 24 hours.
Each hour is 60 minutes long.
It takes about two minutes
to brush your teeth.

On farms or in the
countryside, people
know it's morning
because the rooster
is crowing!

Weeks, months, and years

Longer periods of time are divided into weeks,
months, and years, and even bigger periods!
A millennium is 1,000 years.

December

There are seven days in a week.
Do you know their names?

Sun	Mon	Tues	Wed	Thurs	Fri	Sat

There are around four
weeks in a month.

There are
12 months
in a year.

Height

The word we use to measure how tall things are is height. We can measure the height of anything from the tallest mountain to the smallest creature. Height can be measured in feet and inches or meters and centimeters.

This dotted line shows you where to look on a ruler to see how tall you are.

What things can you think of that are taller than you?

Weight

By weighing an object, we can understand how heavy it is. Weight is usually measured in pounds or kilograms. Weighing things is a really important part of cooking and baking.

The pointer on these scales shows us how much the lemons and limes weigh.

Measuring

Measurements let us **understand** more about different objects and help us **compare** them to one another. What can you measure?

Small

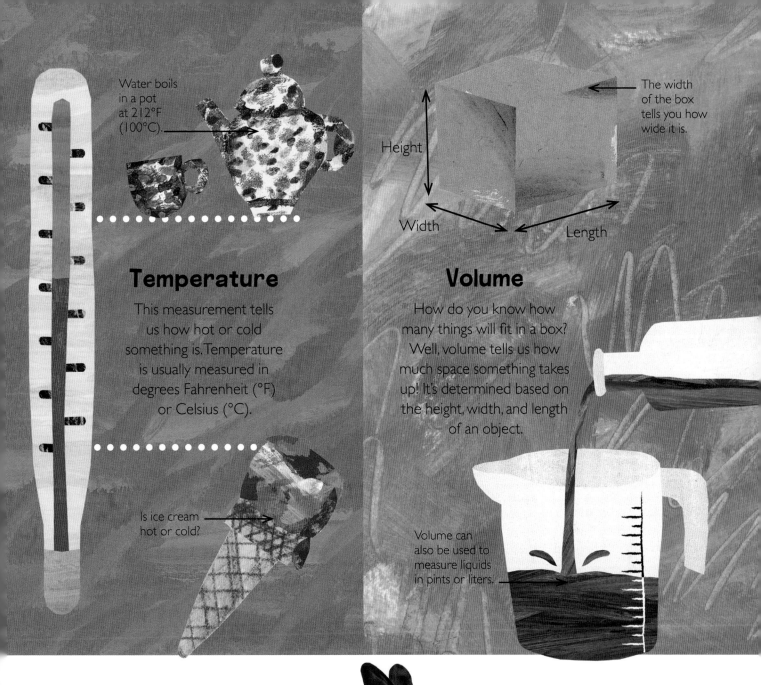

Water boils in a pot at 212°F (100°C).

The width of the box tells you how wide it is.

Height

Width

Length

Temperature

This measurement tells us how hot or cold something is. Temperature is usually measured in degrees Fahrenheit (°F) or Celsius (°C).

Volume

How do you know how many things will fit in a box? Well, volume tells us how much space something takes up! It's determined based on the height, width, and length of an object.

Is ice cream hot or cold?

Volume can also be used to measure liquids in pints or liters.

Medium

Large

Size

Large, medium, and small are words we can use to compare the size of things. What's the largest thing you can think of?

Shapes

Some shapes are **round**, while others are **straight**. There are shapes that are **flat**, and others that are **thick**.

2-D shapes

2-D shapes are flat. They have only a length and a height and are not thick. There are many different 2-D shapes. Can you name any more?

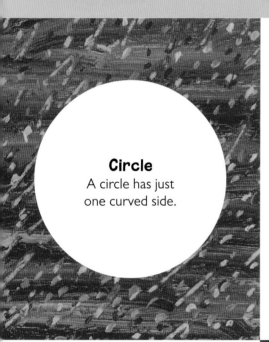

Circle
A circle has just one curved side.

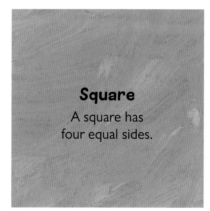

Square
A square has four equal sides.

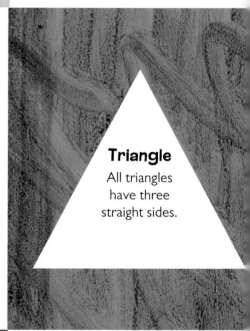

Triangle
All triangles have three straight sides.

Pentagon
This shape has five sides.

Hexagon
This shape has six sides.

Octagon
An octagon has eight sides.

3-D shapes

3-D shapes are thick. They have a length, a height, and a depth. Any shape that is not flat is a 3-D shape. We use lots of 3-D shapes in everyday life.

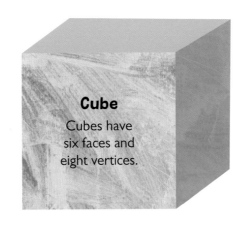

Cube

Cubes have six faces and eight vertices.

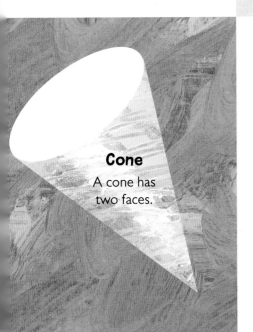

Sphere

A sphere has just one face.

Cylinder

This has three faces.

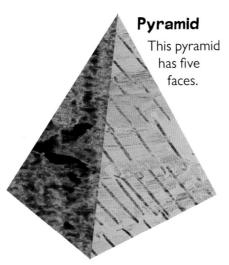

Cone

A cone has two faces.

Pyramid

This pyramid has five faces.

Shapes in the world

Everything around you is made up of lots of different shapes—even this book that you are reading right now! Here are some objects that have different shapes:

This piece of cake is a cube with a sphere on top.

Honeycomb has lots of hexagons.

This ice cream is made up of a cone with a sphere on top.

Symmetry

There are **two types** of symmetry—**reflective** and **rotational**. Symmetry can be seen in many places in the **world around us**.

Reflective symmetry

This type of symmetry shows us how many lines can be drawn to split up a shape into identical parts.

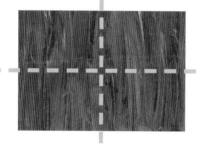

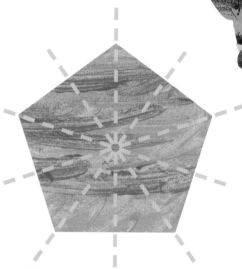

One line of symmetry

This triangle has one line of symmetry. It can be split right down the middle, and each side is exactly the same.

Two lines of symmetry

A rectangle has two lines of symmetry. It can be split vertically or horizontally into identical parts.

More lines of symmetry

Some objects can have many lines of symmetry. This pentagon has five lines of symmetry.

Rotational symmetry

The number of times you can turn an object around and it looks the same is how many degrees of rotational symmetry it has. Here are some examples of rotational symmetry in nature.

This plant has many degrees of symmetry.

This flower can be rotated many times.

This butterfly can be split into two identical parts.

One line of symmetry

Are these images symmetrical?

No! There are also many objects that are not symmetrical at all. We describe these objects as being asymmetrical.

This starfish has five degrees of symmetry.

This clover has three degrees of symmetry.

Space

The universe

Our home is on beautiful planet Earth. Our planet and **everything** around us make up the universe. This includes **stars**, **planets**, **moons**, and lots of empty, dark space.

Our home

Earth is the only planet we know that has living things. Around 8 billion people live here in countries around the world.

Planet Earth

Our planet looks mostly blue because a lot of it is covered in water. The green parts are land.

Solar system

The solar system is our own small part of space, with the sun and eight planets that move around it.

The Big Bang

Scientists believe that everything in our universe started with a big explosion 13.8 billion years ago. The universe was born and has kept growing ever since.

Universe

The universe is everything in space. Beyond the Milky Way, there are billions of other galaxies.

Milky Way

The solar system is part of the Milky Way galaxy. It looks like a gigantic spiral made up of millions of stars and planets.

The solar system

The **sun** is in the **center** of the solar system. The **eight planets** and other smaller objects move around it, including moons and pieces of rock and ice.

Venus
Venus is covered in clouds. It is the hottest planet in the solar system.

Mars
Sometimes known as the "Red Planet," Mars is half the size of Earth.

Mercury
The smallest planet in the solar system is Mercury. It is the closest to the sun.

Earth
Earth is our home and the only planet known to have living things.

Sun
The sun is our closest star. It gives the warmth and light that we need on Earth.

Saturn
Saturn has huge, flat rings made of ice and rock.

Neptune
Neptune is very cold and is the farthest planet from the sun.

Jupiter
Jupiter is the biggest planet and is mostly made of gas.

Uranus
Uranus is the coldest planet and the only one that spins on its side.

Day and night

Over 24 hours, our sky changes from **light to dark**. As it moves from day to night, different creatures **wake and sleep**. Let's see what happens during the day and night...

Daytime

As the sun rises in the morning, a new day begins. The sun gives out light and heat, waking up animals that are active during the day, like us. Birds sing as they make their way to their nests.

We only ever see one side of the moon. The part that is turned away from Earth is called the "dark" side.

Nighttime

Nighttime is when the sun sets, the sky darkens, and we can see the moon and stars shine. Most animals settle down to rest, but some wake up and start to explore, looking for food.

Sun's rays

Night

Day

Why does the sun rise and set?

Every day, Earth spins around once. The half that is facing the sun is in the sun's light, while the other half is in darkness. This creates day and night.

New moon

The face of the moon looks dark during this phase.

Waxing crescent

The moon has moved around the Earth a little. Now we can see the edge hit by sunlight.

First quarter

The moon has moved a quarter of the way around the Earth.

Waxing gibbous

The moon gets bigger each night. This is called waxing.

The magic of the moon

Look up on a clear night and you will see the Earth's closest neighbor in space, the **moon**. Have you ever wondered why it appears to **change shape**? As the moon moves around the Earth each month, different parts are **lit up** by the sun.

Full moon

The moon is now a bright, full circle in the sky!

Waning gibbous

As less of the moon is lit up, we call it waning.

Last quarter

The moon has completed three-quarters of its journey around the Earth.

Waning crescent

We can only see a tiny sliver of moon. Soon it will go dark again.

The moon is almost 250,000 miles (400,000 km) away. It would take about nine and a half years to walk there!

Space rocks

There is a lot more in our vast solar system than just the planets and the sun. There are also smaller pieces of rock floating around. These are made of **metal** and **ice**, as well as **rock**.

Asteroids

Asteroids are lumps of rock tumbling around the sun. There are thousands of them, all in different shapes and sizes.

Meteoroids

When asteroids crash into each other, they make smaller, crumbly rocks called meteoroids.

Space junk

As long as people have been exploring space, they have been leaving behind trash, such as old satellites and pieces of space rocket. Scientists are planning to clean up the mess, before it becomes dangerous for new spacecraft.

Meteors

When space rocks get close to Earth, they burn up and glow. These are called shooting stars, or meteors.

Meteorites

If a space rock crashes into Earth, it can make a hole in the ground called a crater. The rock is now called a meteorite.

Impact!

In the United States, there is a crater where a meteorite crashed into Earth around 50,000 years ago. The hole is as wide as 10 football fields!

A large space rock crater in Arizona

Constellations

The night sky is like an enormous puzzle. For thousands of years, people have looked up and found groups of shapes in the stars. They are called constellations.

The constellation of Cancer is said to look like a giant crab.

When you connect the stars in the Taurus constellation, they look like a charging bull.

Seeing the skies

If you'd like to be a stargazer, you will need the right tools. Telescopes or binoculars make the stars and planets look much closer.

The night sky

Have you ever looked up at the sky at night and noticed the many small, **twinkling** dots? **Stars** are actually giant balls of burning hot gas that are very far away.

The constellation of Pisces represents a pair of fish that share a star at the tail.

The first stargazer

A scientist who studies space is called an astronomer. The first astronomer to use a telescope was an Italian named Galileo Galilei, more than 400 years ago.

Looking to space

Big dish telescope

In China, this massive dish picks up signals from space that might reveal life on other planets.

Reflecting telescope

This huge telescope sits on a mountain in Spain. It uses mirrors to help scientists see stars more clearly.

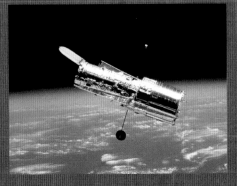

Space telescope

The Hubble Space Telescope circles the Earth about 15 times a day. It has a special camera that takes amazing photos of space.

215

Space travel

Powerful rockets fly into space to **explore** other planets and moons. Sometimes they even carry brave people, called **astronauts**.

First woman in space
Russian cosmonaut Valentina Tereshkova became the first woman in space on June 16, 1963.

1963

Sputnik 1
The first object placed into orbit was Sputnik I, launched in 1957.

1957

1942

1961

German V-2 Rocket
On October 3, 1942, the V-2 missile was the first rocket launched into space.

First man in space
Russian cosmonaut Yuri Gagarin was the first person to travel into space.

Russian space explorers are called cosmonauts.

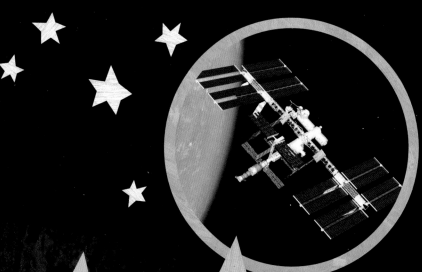

International Space Station (ISS)

Construction of the ISS began in 1998. It is a home and workplace for astronauts in space.

1969

1998

2012

2019

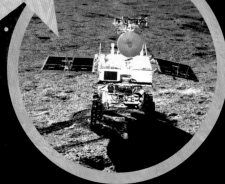

Curiosity Rover on Mars

In 2012, the Curiosity Rover became the largest robotic vehicle to land on Mars.

China's Chang'e 4

On January 2, 2019, China landed a rover on the far side of the moon. China also landed a rover, called Zhurong, on Mars in 2021.

First people on the moon

In 1969, American astronauts Neil Armstrong and Buzz Aldrin were the first people to step on the moon.

The space race

Throughout the 1960s, the Soviet Union and the United States competed to be the first country to send a person to the moon. In 1969, the US achieved the first moon landing.

This postage stamp celebrates the launching of two spacecraft by the Soviet Union.

The first landing on the moon by the US is honored in this postage stamp.

Glossary

2-D shapes
Flat shapes that have a length and a height

3-D shapes
Thick shapes that have a length, a height, and a depth

acceleration
When something moves faster and faster

art gallery
Place where works of art are shown and can be viewed by the public

atom
Smallest part of a solid, liquid, or gas

camouflage
Animals' coloring or pattern that allows them to blend in with their surroundings, so they cannot be easily seen

circuit
Loop made of wires that electricity can flow through

compass
Object that helps people find their way around by showing directions

coniferous
Type of tree that stays green all year round

continent
Large area of land, such as Asia or Africa

coral reef
Rocklike structure made up of groups of tiny sea animals called corals. Coral reefs are often found along coastlines

crater
Large hole in the ground made by the impact from a space rock

deciduous
Type of tree that loses its leaves in the fall

desert
Area of land where it hardly ever rains

earthquake
Movements on the surface of the Earth that make the ground shake

electricity
Type of energy that can provide power to electrical objects, such as a toaster

energy
Source of power, such as light energy or electrical energy

festival
Celebration or special event, often with dancing and music

force
Push or pull that affects the way an object moves

fossil
Remains or traces of an ancient animal or plant

friction
Force that slows down moving things

gravity
Force that pulls objects toward each other

magnetism
Force used by magnets to push or pull other objects

minerals
Substances found in rocks and soil

mountain range
Collection of mountains grouped together

muscle
Part of the body that helps you to move

nocturnal animals
Animals that sleep during the day and are awake at night

North Pole
Northernmost point on Earth

organ
Part of the body that does a specific job. For example, your lungs help you breathe

particles
Tiny parts of a solid, liquid, or gas

photosynthesis
Process by which plants make their food

planet
Large, round object in space that moves around a star

predator
Animal that hunts and eats other animals

prehistoric
Ancient time before recorded history

prey
Animal that is hunted and eaten by another animal

recycle
Turning a waste object into something new

savanna
Large area of flat grassland usually found in hot countries

season
Period of weather during the year, such as summer or winter

senses
Things that make you aware of the world, such as smell, taste, and sight

sound wave
How sound travels through the air

South Pole
Southernmost point on Earth

symmetry
When two halves of a shape match each other

telescope
Tool that makes faraway objects, such as planets, appear closer than they are

tropical
Area or climate with high rainfall and hot temperatures

vibration
Back and forth movement

volcano
Huge mountain filled with hot rock called magma that sometimes erupts

X-ray
Special image that shows the inside of your body

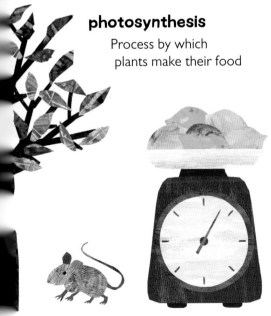

Index

Index

Acknowledgments

The World of Eric Carle nurtures a child's love of literature and learning, encouraging imaginative play and exploration. Trusted by parents, teachers, and librarians and beloved by children worldwide for generations, *The Very Hungry Caterpillar* and other timeless storybooks come to life in colorfully creative books and products, designed to inspire very hungry young minds. Eric Carle is acclaimed and beloved as the creator of brilliantly illustrated and innovatively designed picture books for very young children. Carle illustrated more than 70 books, many best-sellers, most of which he also wrote, and more than 170 million copies of his books have sold around the world. *The Very Hungry Caterpillar's Very First Encyclopedia* covers these important early learning topics:

Our world

Body and health

Earth

Animals and nature

History

Science, math, and technology

Space

DK would like to thank Romi Chakraborty, Kanika Kalra, Vijay Khandwal, Bhagyashree Nayak, Balwant Singh, and Dheeraj Singh for their design and DTP assistance; Aditya Katyal, Vagisha Pushp, and Sakshi Saluja for picture research help; Elle Ward for design help; Mark Clifton for additional illustrations; Marie Greenwood, Kieran Jones, Abi Luscombe, Manisha Majithia, and Seeta Parmar for editorial help; Caroline Hunt for proofreading; and Helen Peters for the index.

The publisher would like to thank the following for their kind permission to reproduce their photographs:

(Key: a-above; b-below/bottom; c-center; f-far; l-left; r-right; t-top)

1 123RF.com: leonello calvetti (br). **Dorling Kindersley:** Natural History Museum, London (cb). Dreamstime.com: Mitgirl (cra). **8** Dreamstime.com: Günter Albers (bc/forest); Oksanaphoto (br). Getty Images / iStock: Peter Llewellyn (bc). **9 Dreamstime.com:** Madrabothair (br); Dongli Zhang (bc/City); Alexander Ovchinnikov (bc). **10** 123RF.com: imagesource (cra). **11 Getty Images:** DigitalVision / Jose Luis Pelaez Inc (cla). **12 Alamy Stock Photo:** Stephen R. Johnson (bl). **Getty Images / iStock:** E+ / eli_asenova (tr). **Shutterstock.com:** ToeFoTo (c). **13 Alamy Stock Photo:** Design Pics / Radius Images (cr). **Dreamstime.com:** Kiankhoon (tc). **14 Dreamstime.com:** Ajn (tr). **Fotolia:** Yahia Loukkal (cl). **15 Dreamstime.com:** Bjorn Heller / Dr3amer (tr). **16 Dreamstime.com:** Slavun (b). **17 Dreamstime.com:** Dvilfruit (bl). NASA: JPL-Caltech (tr). **18-19 Dreamstime.com:** Slawomir Kruz. **19 Dreamstime.com:** David Burke (cla); Eugenesergeev (cb). **21 Dreamstime.com:** Williammacgregor (bc). **22 Dreamstime.com:** Scott Dumas (bc/Kimono). **Getty Images / iStock:** E+ / hadynyah (bc); Nikhil Patil (br). **23 Alamy Stock Photo:** Ton Koene (br). **Dreamstime.com:** Kdshutterman (cra); Moti Meiri (fcra); Toxitz (tr). **Getty Images**

/ iStock: E+ / hadynyah (bl); loonger (bc). **24 Alamy Stock Photo:** Oleksiy Maksymenko Photography (clb); Sean Pavone (tc). Dreamstime.com: Jan Wachala (br). **Shutterstock.com:** Cenap Refik Ongan (cra). **25 Alamy Stock Photo:** Ian Dagnall (crb). **Dreamstime.com:** Anekoho (tl); Sergii Sverdielov (cra); Resul Muslu (bl). **Getty Images:** Jasmin Merdan (cb). **26 123RF.com:** Martin Damen (bc). Dreamstime.com: Hanhanpeggy (cla); Gino Santa Maria (clb). **27 Dreamstime.com:** Digikhmer (bl); Phive2015 (tc); J33p3l2 (cla); Tomert (br). **28 Dreamstime.com:** Mreco99 (cra). **28-29 Shutterstock.com:** bioraven (bc). 29 123RF. com: aimy27feb (bl). **Dreamstime.com:** Irina88w / © Successió Miró / ADAGP, Paris and DACS London 2021 (ca). **30 Dreamstime.com:** Riccardo Lennart Niels Mayer (bl); Vtupinamba (cl); Ppy2010ha (c). **31** 123RF.com: Baiba Opule (cra). **Dreamstime.com:** Gekaskr (tr); Robyn Mackenzie (clb). **Getty Images / iStock:** filipefrazao (bc); somethingway (tl). **32 Getty Images / iStock:** XtockImages (br). **33** 123RF. com: gresei (clb). **Dreamstime.com:** Ryan Pike (fbr); Yi Min Zhu (bc). **Getty Images / iStock:** bong hyunjung (br). **34 Dreamstime.com:** Artranq (tc); Olga Besnard (c); Elena Chepik (cr). **35 Alamy Stock Photo:** Newscom / BJ Warnick (ca). **Dreamstime.com:** Crackerclips (bl); Alina Shpak (cl); Pamela Uyttendaele (cb); Sergiy Nigeruk (bc); Magdalena Żurawska (br). **Shutterstock.com:** Top Photo Engineer (tl). **37 Alamy Stock Photo:** Joerg Boethling (tr). **39 123RF.com:** Kuznetsov Dmitry (cra); Rob Marmion (br). **Dreamstime.com:** Prasit Rodphan (c). **40** 123RF.com: utima (cla). **Getty Images / iStock:** SciePro (cr). **43 Getty Images / iStock:** E+ / kali9 (crb). **44 Getty Images / iStock:** SciePro (br). **45 Dreamstime.com:** Itsmejust (br). **Shutterstock.com:** Manny DaCunha (bl). **46** 123RF.com: utima (cra). **47 Getty Images:** Jill Fromer / Photodisc (cr). **48 Dreamstime.com:** Shao-chun Wang (cr). **Shutterstock.com:** ShotPrime Studio (cr). **49 Alamy Stock Photo:** Image Source / David Jakle (cr). **Getty Images / iStock:** E+ / Kemter (c); E+ / izusek (clb). **54 Alamy Stock Photo:** Stephen Frost (cb); KQS (crb). **55 Alamy Stock**

Photo: Oleksiy Maksymenko Photography (crb). **Dreamstime.com:** Brizmaker (clb); Witold Korczewski (tl). **Getty Images:** Nichola Evans / Photodisc (cb). **57** 123RF.com: ferli (cla); pixelrobot (clb). Depositphotos Inc: zurijeta (b). **Dreamstime.com:** Chernetskaya (cra); Mitgirl (cl). 59 123RF.com: anmbph (tl). **Dreamstime. com:** Tom Wang (tr). **61 Dreamstime.com:** Alexandra Karamysheva (tl). 62 **Dreamstime. com:** Vacclav (cl). **Getty Images / iStock:** gustavofrazao (cb). **63 Dreamstime.com:** Denis Belitskiy (tl); Ivan Kmit / Ivankmit (cra); Hel080808 (cb). **64 Dreamstime.com:** Elenatur (clb). **65 Alamy Stock Photo:** Novarc Images / Dennis Schmelz / mauritius images GmbH (c). **Dreamstime.com:** Caoerlei (tc). **66 Alamy Stock Photo:** Nature Picture Library (tc). **Getty Images:** Michele Falzone (br). **67 Dreamstime. com:** Adriel80 (crb); Diana Dunlap (bl). **68** 123RF.com: sugarwarrior (bc). Dreamstime. com: Surangaw (ca). **69 Dreamstime.com:** Vladimir Melnikov (tr); Tomas1111 (cr). **70 Dreamstime.com:** Agap13 (cb); Ghm Meuffels / Gerardmeuffels (ca). **71 Dreamstime.com:** Luis Leamus (tr). Getty Images / iStock: Byrdyak (crb). **72 Alamy Stock Photo:** Kevin Schafer / Avalon.red (bl). 73 Alamy Stock Photo: Alain Grosclaude (cr). **Dreamstime.com:** Tolly81 (tr). 76 Dreamstime.com: Pablo Hidalgo (tc). **77 Alamy Stock Photo:** Per-Andre Hoffmann / Image Professionals GmbH (cra). **Dreamstime. com:** (cr); Gagarych (ca); Ralf Lehmann (cb). **Getty Images:** Huoguangliang (crb). **80 Dreamstime.com:** Paul Hampton (cr); Alexey Poprotskiy (cra). **81 Dreamstime.com:** Soloway (c). **83** 123RF.com: (crb). **Dreamstime.com:** Photosvit (cb). **84** 123RF.com: Iurii Buriak (bc). **Alamy Stock Photo:** Ben Pipe (tr). **85 Alamy Stock Photo:** Allgöwer Walter / Prisma by Dukas Presseagentur GmbH (bl); Image Professionals GmbH / Jörg Reuther (tl); Sébastien Lecocq (tr). **Dreamstime.com:** Beehler (bc). **86 Alamy Stock Photo:** Jan Wlodarczyk (br). **Dreamstime.com:** Helen Hotson (bl). **87 Dorling Kindersley:** Natural History Museum, London (cra, cr, cb); University of Pennsylvania Museum of Archaeology and Anthropology (bl); Oxford University Museum of Natural History (c, crb). **Dreamstime.com:** Nastya81 (cl).